MW00700851

The Paris Way

# of Beauty

THE PARIS

Illustrations by Nancy Stahl
Photographs by Didier Massard

WAY of BEAUTY

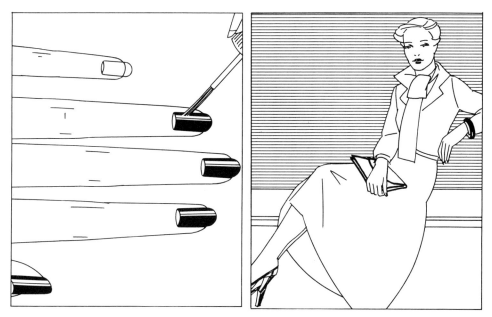

By Linda Dannenberg

SIMON AND SCHUSTER • NEW YORK

Copyright © 1978, 1979 by Linda Dannenberg

All rights reserved
including the right of reproduction
in whole or in part in any form
Published by Simon and Schuster
A Division of Gulf & Western Corporation
Simon & Schuster Building
Rockefeller Center
1230 Avenue of the Americas
New York, New York 10020

Manufactured in the United States of America

1 2 3 4 5 6 7 8 9 10

Library of Congress Cataloging in Publication Data

Dannenberg, Linda.
  The Paris way of beauty.
  1. Beauty, Personal. 2. Beauty shops—France—
Paris—Directories. I. Title.
RA778.D244   646.7′2   79-4241
ISBN 0-671-24723-9

Grateful acknowledgment is made to *Family Circle* magazine for its kind permission to reprint material from my article "Beauty Secrets from the Great Paris Salons," © by Family Circle, Inc., 1978.

Material from my column "Looking Good" is reprinted with permission from *Working Woman* magazine, © by WW Publications, 1977.

Special thanks to the following companies and publications for permission to use photographs by Didier Massard: jacket, right, Harriet Hubbard Ayer-Paris, makeup by Olivier Echaudemaison; page 40, *Jacinte;* pages 69, 171, 185, *Marie France;* pages 57, 83, 91, 101, 107, *Vogue France;* page 119, *Marie Claire.*

To my mother and father,
with appreciation and love

Acknowledgments

This book was a project that involved many people. I gratefully acknowledge the generous cooperation of the Paris salons and *instituts de beauté;* the book would not have been possible without them. I would like to thank Arthur Hettich and Maxine Lewis at *Family Circle* magazine, where parts of this book originally appeared in a slightly different form, for their early enthusiasm and support. I would also like to thank the following people, each of whom, in his or her own special way, helped me: Alice Allen, Frédéric de Broglie, Joni Evans, Nives Falcioni and Norbert, Alan Kahn, Ted L'Ourson, La Verne Powlis, Connie Schrader, Esther and Christian Viros and Françoise Wernert.

CONTENTS

THE PARIS WAY

# of BEAUTY

I
INTRODUCTION

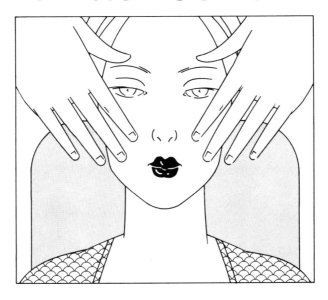

When Paris talks beauty, the rest of the world listens. Because when it comes to beauty care, Paris is incomparable—for quantity of services, for originality of ideas and for quality of care. In this enchantingly lovely, sophisticated town of wide boulevards, graceful bridges and sublime architecture, there are more salons, more *instituts de beauté* and more specialized beauty treatments than anywhere else. Paris is The Source; here the world's most innovative cosmetic ideas are conceived, as are the latest trends in body care, hairstyle and skin treatment. The phrase "new from Paris" linked with a product or style virtually guarantees an advertiser or promoter anywhere on the globe instant success.

This Mecca of beauty, where cosmetic and esthetic treatments are considered an art, fascinated me. What was it that made Paris so special in this field? Why was the city, if not the entire country, so preoccupied with cosmetic and esthetic beauty? And why, for heaven's sake, did the women look so *good*—meticulous, trim, elegant, polished—the quintessence of the word *soignée*? It couldn't *all* be in the genes. What did they know that I didn't? What were they doing to themselves or what were the salons and *instituts* doing for them? Were Parisian cosmetologists and stylists superior to their counterparts outside La Belle France?

1. Claude Maxime Salon
2. Jean-Pierre Fleurimon Centre de Beauté
3. Jacques Clemente/Elizabeth Arden
4. Isabelle Lancray Institut de Beauté
5. Patrick Alès Salon
6. Guerlain
7. Alexandre
8. Ingrid Millet Institut de Beauté
9. Carita

10. Clarins
11. Institut des Jambes
12. Maigrir, Rester Mince
13. Institut Payot
14. Luis Llongueras Salon
15. Herbier de Provence
16. Louis G. Salon
17. Béatrice Braun Institut de Beauté
18. Jean-Marc Maniatis Salon

It seemed to me that the French had kept their beauty secrets to themselves long enough. The time had come for the rest of us to profit by their know-how. So, I set aside several months, as well as a large pile of francs and centimes, and embarked for Paris to explore the great beauty establishments. I went to be cared for in the best places, to meet and talk to the experts and trend setters, to observe the Parisian women in their natural habitat. In short, I went to learn how to be beautiful *à la française*.

It quickly became apparent to me that the French take beauty care very seriously; it is a respected area of study and an honored profession. The requirements for practicing in any area of the beauty field are stringent. And, not surprisingly, the quality of beauty care is high. Although always on the lookout for new and more effective *soins du corps* (body treatments) and *soins du visage* (facial treatments), the Paris salons and *instituts* are extremely conscientious in their approach to beauty care; most owners work in conjunction with doctors to develop their techniques and products. Over and over again I heard Paris beauty care described as "paramedical": treatments are therapeutic rather than simply cosmetic. Many specialists in the beauty field must have some medical background to be licensed. For example, the only pedicures allowed in Paris are "medical" pedicures. A pedicurist, the equivalent here of a chiropodist, must attend a medical school or train in a hospital for two years, and then pass a state exam, before being allowed to give a pedicure in a salon.

I was amazed to learn the prerequisites to become an *esthéticienne*—a person who specializes in skin and facial care. First she must either (1) have completed a two-year course in a professional or trade school, or (2) have a diploma from one of the special *esthéticiennes* schools offering intensive, year-long preparatory courses, or (3) complete a several-years-long apprenticeship combined with the successful completion of correspondence courses. Then she must pass the grueling CAP (Certificat d'Aptitude Professionnelle) examination. The exam is divided into two parts over two days. The first day encompasses a written examination which lasts from 7:30 in the morning until 5:30 in the afternoon. This comprehensive exam includes questions on mathematical problems, commerce, French law, "household education," anatomy, the history of makeup through the ages, psychology, skin characteristics, skin disorders and diseases, chemistry as related to cosmetic products and, of course, function and use of apparatus. There is also a design section where the candidate is asked to draw the twent-six facial muscles, identifying their points of origin and their functions.

On the second day of the exam the candidates demonstrate their practical skills. To the exam they must bring their own models and their own professionally equipped makeup kits. First they are asked to demonstrate their facial treatment techniques for different skin types. Then they are told to do a specialized makeup—it could be a wedding makeup, a formal evening makeup or perhaps a theatrical makeup such as a witch or a clown. After this the candidates perform a manicure on their models. In the final section of the exam they must analyze the skin of a stranger, evaluate the problems and recommend treatment. Only after passing the two-part CAP exam is a person allowed to give a facial in France.

Now look at the requirements for a cosmetologist in the United States. The laws are a little different in every state, but let's take New York as an example. In order to earn a Diploma of Hairdressing and Cosmetology (one diploma covers both), a candidate must offer proof of having attended 1,000 hours of a hairdressing or beauty school (30 hours of which concern skin), pass a written examination consisting of 100 multiple-choice questions, less than 10 of which are on skin, and pass a practical examination, based on hair only, where the candidate must demonstrate the techniques for comb-outs, roller sets, permanents, finger waves, hair lightening and hair straightening. Every person who passes this exam is allowed to work on your skin and face. When you compare the French qualifications for becoming a certified *esthéticienne* with the American ones for becoming a licensed cosmetologist, you have a clear answer why beauty care in France is superior.

I noted that French women schedule visits to their local beauty establishments much more frequently than their American sisters, particularly for facial and skin-related care. The salon facial is a regular monthly activity for most, sometimes scheduled even more often for those with problems. As soon as a skin problem presents itself—be it blackheads, unusually dry skin or acne—*la Française* hies herself imme-

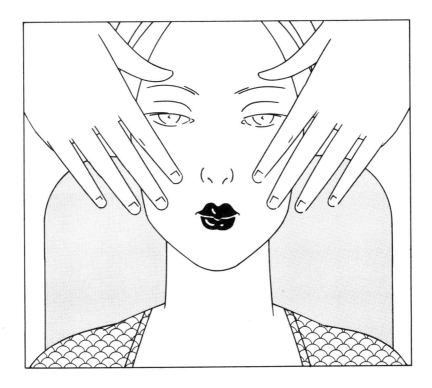

diately to her local *esthéticienne*, and only afterward, if need be, to the dermatologist. She would never let it go, hoping it would disappear of its own accord.

The French are more appearance-conscious than we are, for all our emphasis on exercise and proper diet. The women tend their bodies like works of art, keeping them as free as possible from signs of aging. After talking to and observing many French women in order to learn why they take such care with themselves—is it pride? health? tradition?—I've come up with several answers. "We're very vain," Nicole Arbour, a Parisienne formerly with Carita and now transplanted in New York as partner at the Yves Claude Salon, told me. "We wouldn't even go out for a newspaper or to the *boulangerie* without making sure we look well. Because we're worried about what the gossip-loving neighbors will say. If we went out in sloppy pants, or no makeup, like women do here, our ears would burn—'Did you see *that* one today? She looks like the handyman. . . .' or 'Oh, la, la, she certainly looks her age without makeup.'" Another major consideration is the opposite sex; the French

The French woman is one of the most individualistic in the world.

woman works hard to keep her face smooth, her skin soft, her body slim and her hands and feet well-groomed, to attract, please and keep men. "We have to be on our toes all the time," said Madame Arbour. "Men are always looking at other women. We feel the competition." In many ways French women are less "liberated" than we are, but to use a French expression, *elles s'en fichent*—they don't give a damn. They spend time on themselves to look good for their men, and they make apologies to no one for their priorities.

Of course, tradition and pride also play a part also, in contributing to the French preoccupation with beauty. In an interview I had with Isabelle Lancray, president of the Fédération Française de l'Esthétique-Cosmétique and for twenty-eight years the *directrice* of her own salon, I asked why she thought beauty care was so important to the French.

"Beauty is an ancestral vocation," she told me, "which has come down to us through the centuries. The French have always been great admirers of beauty in all forms, be it physical, pure art such as painting and sculpture, jewelry or fashion. All of these areas of art and beauty cross-pollinate each other and creativity blooms. Because of so many years of permanent contact with beauty in all its manifestations, a trained eye is developed and a certain taste formed. It's only natural, given this background, that the French should care so deeply about beauty care, and that Paris, where artists of genius convene, should be its source."

On the French woman, Madame Lancray is direct and succinct: "The French woman is one of the most individualistic in the world. She doesn't want to resemble anyone else. She is very demanding, and always on the lookout for things that will help her feel *bien dans sa peau*—good within herself."

The majority of women who frequent the salons and *instituts* of Paris are generally not the super-rich with time on their hands and money to burn, although you do see the occasional princess or heiress passing through. Rather, the women who make up the largest percentage of the Parisian clientele are women who work, or middle-income housewives who schedule their visits while the children are in school. Most clients are in the thirty-to-sixty-year-old bracket, although there are some as young as fifteen, others as old as eighty. For many of these women the twenty to fifty dollars a month they spend on treatments is a sacrifice, or at least a noticeable pinch in the pocketbook. But the tariffs for beauty treatments are considered a necessary expense, not an extravagance. The benefits are psychological as well as physical. An hour spent receiving the undivided attention of a trained beauty specialist, whose only concern is to make your face and body look and feel good, does wonders for your ego and morale. It's an hour of pure "me." Judging from the look of well-being and contentment of the women leaving the salons, as well as from my own experience, I would venture to say that a visit to an *institut* is more than worth the price of admission.

Before I go any further, I should briefly explain the difference between a salon and an *institut de beauté*. Salons are generally for hair care and makeup, occasionally for facials, but never for body treatments. *Instituts de beauté* are mainly for body treatments and facials, sometimes for makeup, but never for hairstyling. The line between the two tends to be a little fuzzy, and I will occasionally use the word "salon" to cover all beauty establishments.

The salons and *instituts* of Paris vary greatly in their approach to beauty and in their degree of specialization. Some establishments, such as Carita, offer comprehensive beauty care; others are extremely specialized, building their reputations on treatments for breasts or hands or legs or skin. The owners of the salons and *instituts*, some of whom are world-renowned, range from young, flamboyant experimentalists to classic, revered traditionalists. I chose the establishments I visited in several ways. Some I had heard about for years—their names were in travel guidebooks like *Fielding's* and *Fodor's*, in fashion magazines like *Vogue* and *Harper's Bazaar*, and in newspapers like the *New York Times* and the *San Francisco Chronicle*, where owners were quoted as experts. Others I picked up from reading a year's worth of French beauty magazines. And still others I learned about through word of mouth while I was in Paris. Almost everyone I spoke to had a "must" for me to visit. It was difficult to narrow the field to the twenty or so salons and *instituts* I focused on*; in Paris alone there are over 400 *instituts de beauté*

---

*The salons and *instituts* described below are the establishments where I spent the most time, or received the most information. Several others will appear from time to time throughout the text. A complete listing of all the salons, *instituts de beauté*, and experts mentioned in this book appears in the Appendix.

and almost 5,000 hairdressers. I decided on the places that had the best reputations, as well as a little something extra that appealed to me—a style, a philosophy, a certain clientele, an unusual product line or a particularly creative, spirited artist.

Carita, the famous, trend-setting and very busy salon, sits near the tip of Paris's most expensive shopping street at 11 rue du Faubourg Saint-Honoré. The salon, a white and chrome, multi-leveled establishment, was founded by the two Carita sisters, Rosy and the late Maria, who came to Paris from Toulouse in the early forties. Their nephew, Christophe, known for his super-elegant chignons, is the artist in the house, designing and executing new styles every season. Carita is a beauty *institut* as well as a hair and makeup salon, where facial and various types of body treatments are given. There is also a men's salon, Carita Monsieur, offering hair care and skin care to the male of the species.

Carita is a favorite of the international set—royalty, actresses, heiresses. Catherine Deneuve is a frequent client, as are Marisa Berenson and Isabelle Adjani. While I waited for a makeup session, a young woman came out of one of the treatment rooms and proceeded down to the hairdressing floor. The receptionist picked up the phone, dialed and said, "Tell them the Baroness Rothschild is on her way."

Alexandre, a true virtuoso of hairstyling, is considered by many to be the master of masters. He's been in the business for forty years, and still works daily in his elegant burgundy and peach salon at 120 rue du Faubourg Saint-Honoré, dispensing superb cuts and beauty counsel to his faithful clientele. Customers include Princess Grace and Princess Caroline of Monaco, who reflect his style of simple elegance. Twice a year Alexandre, a dapper man with wavy grey hair, a trim moustache and a gallant manner, does the hair of the mannequins who appear in the great collections—Dior, Saint-Laurent, Givenchy. Here Alexandre is wonderfully creative, wrapping, twisting, weaving and wildly accessorizing his new styles, almost always making news in the world of *haute couture*.

The mood *chez* Alexandre is calm and quiet, with relaxed, smiling clients. This is a marked difference from the bustle and frenetic pace of some other Paris salons where the women wait and wait, none too happily. Alexandre communicates his views on women and beauty with missionary zeal. "My role is to bring out an individual's beauty and teach her how to keep it," he says. "I am strict and direct with my women and the advice I give them, to help them look as good as they possibly can."

At the exquisite **Institut Guerlain,** at 68 avenue des Champs-Élysées, I found the Paris beauty salon of my imagination: a grand reception room with crystal chandeliers, Oriental rugs, Louis XV-style furnishings and an atmosphere of tranquility and refinement. To add to the dreamy setting, the delicious scent of Guerlain perfume floats in the air. Guerlain is renowned for its manicures, performed in the splendor of the mahogany-walled, crystal-sconced grand salon, and you must book weeks in advance for an appointment. The house of Guerlain also gives fine facials, makeups, pedicures, *épilations* (removal of unwanted hair) and massage. Before leaving the salon after an appointment, each client is sprayed with a cloud of her favorite Guerlain perfume. You walk away from Guerlain feeling pampered and supremely feminine.

Béatrice Braun, a warm and welcoming woman who, in her mid-thirties looks like a schoolgirl, is one of the youngest salon owners in Paris. Her attractive, modern *institut*, decorated in beiges and browns with soft, indirect lighting and accents of polished chrome, is at 39 rue de Sèvres, in a chic, boutique-filled area of the Left Bank. Madame Braun's *institut* features health-oriented, complete body care, with all treatments monitored by her physician husband. Dr. Marcel Braun, a doctor in general medicine, practiced in Paris for eighteen years before he decided to devote himself full-time to the *institut*, consulting with new clients as well as directing all laboratory research and development of products. The Institut Braun is currently researching products that can reinforce the skin's connective tissue (the layer of skin where wrinkles form), using collagen, elastin and silicone, components that make up the connective fibers. The *institut* is noted for its anticellulite treatments and its specialized massages. But perhaps the best reason for going to the Institut Braun is to meet and talk with Béatrice, one of the nicest people I met while I was in Paris.

The new Institut **Ingrid Millet,** set in an old courtyard at 54 rue du Faubourg Saint-Honoré, is full of natural light and green plants. It's a refreshing oasis in the middle of town. Madame Millet is a petite, elegant woman of "just sixty," she says proudly, because she doesn't look within ten years of it. Her products are nature-based, with many originating from the sea—creams, lotions and masks from oysters, caviar, algae and sea mud, said to be rich in minerals and proteins, with some antibiotic properties. Ingrid Millet did not begin her career as an *esthéticienne* until the age of forty, when she had to go back to work after divorcing her husband. Her *institut* is now one of the most popular in Paris.

A serious *institut* with ninety branches in Europe, the **Institut des Jambes** (Institute for Legs) was opened in 1963 by a group of doctors, phlebologists to be precise, who founded the *institut* specifically for the treatment of leg problems—varicose veins, broken capillaries and cellulite. The Paris *institut*, in a marbled office building at 87 rue Saint-Lazare, is the seat of the operation. The *directrice* is Madame Delille, a reserved, carefully coiffed woman who worked for fifteen years as a research assistant for the founders prior to the opening of the *institut*. The unique *Frigibas* varicose vein treatment, a specialty of the house, is sanctioned by the French board of health, and has been patented in the United States. The Institut des Jambes was the most medically oriented establishment I visited; their work is therapeutic primarily, cosmetic only as a side benefit.

Clarins is a total body-care *institut*, but it is perhaps best known for its breast-care treatments and products. The Paris *institut*, newly decorated in shades of pure white and burnt orange, is in an attractive, remodeled building at 35 rue Tronchet, the popular shopping street behind the Place de la Madeleine. Clarins was founded in 1955 by Jacques Courtin, a genial, smiling man who began his career as a physical therapist. It is M. Courtin who developed all the products and treatments, and who continues to direct the entire operation, which today comprises 120 branches all over Europe and South America. The *institut*, which was being expanded while I was there to accommodate its growing clientele, enjoys a solid reputation.

The **Isabelle Lancray Institut de Beauté,** founded twenty-eight years ago by the dynamic Isabelle Lancray, and located at 29 rue François Ier, is one of the earliest established salons still operating successfully in Paris. The rooms have a slightly rococo look, with yellow and muted green trompe l'oeil walls, elaborate chandeliers and graceful, carved armchairs placed around the foyer. One spacious, airy room is a hairdressing salon. In another area are the treatment cabins where facials, *épilations* and other body treatments are performed. The *institut*, today run by *directrice*

Perrine Pultz, is particularly well known for its special neck and under-eye techniques.

At the **Patrick Alès** salon you can have your hair treated with a specially created line of 100 percent natural products, made from exotic plants found in Provence and in parts of Africa. M. Alès, the stocky, bearded owner, who never wears anything but a black Nehru suit, is a hair-care zealot. "There is no such thing as bad hair," he says, "only badly cared-for hair." He devoted fifteen years to developing his *phytothérapie* (plant-based care) products, whose ingredients include henna, kaolin, soapwort and nasturtiums. The star *coiffeur* in residence is Romain, a young, creative super-stylist, 50 percent of whose time is spent coiffing models for magazine covers. Jacqueline Onassis, Racquel Welch and Holland's Queen Juliana are among the notable clients of this modern, pleasant salon at 35 avenue Franklin Roosevelt, just off the Champs-Élysées.

Jean-Marc Maniatis is one of the most important young *coiffeurs* in Paris. His three bustling salons, with headquarters at 35 rue de Sèvres, are full of models, trendy young women and arty-looking matrons. His signature style is the short, free and easy cut. Jean-Marc spent years working exclusively with fashion magazines, coiffing models in styles that were often new and outrageous. He seems to have an innate sense about just when women are ready for a change, and is usually the front-runner of the newest trends in hair design.

Maigrir, Rester Mince, whose name means "Lose Weight, Stay Thin," is an *institut* which concerns itself exclusively with weight and volume reduction. "We treat deformed silhouettes," says co-director Ferdinand Goyetche. Women inscribe themselves for a three-and-a-half-week "cure," which consists of consultations and treatments at the *institut* combined with a strict, well-balanced diet to be followed at home. The client is seen every two days during the program, which is supervised by two doctors. Maigrir, Rester Mince, at 46 rue Blanche, is a duplex of offices and treatment rooms in north-central Paris. The style is sober and comfortable, more like a dentist's office than an *institut de beauté*.

At 4 rue de Bourgogne, one block from the Seine in a charming residential section of the Left Bank, **Louis G.** coifs women who have an air of quiet wealth and class about them. The salon is tiny, and feels very private. Friendly, white-haired Monsieur G. greets everyone personally, exchanging kisses on both cheeks with some of his favored customers. For hair care he prefers natural treatments, using beef marrow, eggs and lemon juice, followed by a beautiful cut, designed to be worn unfettered during the day, pulled back with combs at cocktail hour and drawn into a chignon for a gala evening out.

The shaggy-haired, Spanish **Luis Llongueras** does some of the most innovative hairstyles in town. His clients leave the contemporary salon at 229 rue Saint-Honoré with striking asymmetrical or graduated cuts, wispy, delicate permanents without frizz or unusual short/long combination cuts. Always on the lookout for styles and techniques to simplify hair care for women, Llongueras, who also runs five successful salons in Spain, comes up with unique results in an experimental, avant-garde mode.

In doing research for this book, I was cared for and pampered the way the very rich are. I went to a salon or *institut de beauté* almost every day, sometimes twice a day. I was made up, styled, massaged, pedicured, waxed and facialed by the world's best. I let the beauty experts and artists have a free hand with me, to see how they would interpret my "look," without my own preconceived notions to guide them. My one fear—that after four months of salon-hopping and "makeovers" every few weeks, I would return home with one millimeter left of my shoulder-length hair and eyebrows tweezed to nothingness—did not come to pass. I discovered early on that if a beauty artist thought something was right to begin with, he didn't alter it simply for the sake of change.

I was open to all kinds of new treatments, ready for unusual techniques and personal idiosyncracies, expecting a variety of decors and clientele. But there was one aspect of the Paris salons for which I was not prepared: the dogs. Women bring their dogs, large and small, with them, and the animals are expected to wait obediently while their mistresses are coiffed and primped. I saw a woman having her hair streaked while her enormous boxer dog sat placidly by her side, watching. Occasionally, I was told, there are problems with dogfights. When I asked the Carita press representative why big dogs were allowed in their salon, she responded, surprised at the question, "Why, if you don't bring them, where can they go?"

One of the most important things I learned from my visits to the Paris beauty establishments was that you don't *have* to go to a salon or *institut de beauté* to care for yourself properly. Much of what is done in the beauty houses, you can do at home, if you know how, and take the time to do it. The major difference is that it won't be done *to* you (admittedly a very pleasant part of the experience). Of course not everything can be done at home. You should visit a good hairdresser at least every six weeks for a trim or restyling, and have a facial, if there's a facial salon in your area, every month to six weeks for a deep pore cleansing.

The most valuable bit of advice I can give you, as you begin this book, is to be open to change. Do not be kept from looking as good as you can look by a frozen image of yourself. Experiment. Try new looks, new colors, new treatments. You will only be improved by it. As Alexandre told me, "Do not be too easily satisfied with your appearance, when with a little more effort you could look so much better."

35

II
Your Skin

The Paris beauty houses, always on the lookout for new, natural ways to keep skin clean, healthy and young, offer a wide range of specialized treatments in addition to the basic monthly facial. Treatments can be rather exotic: some women inscribe themselves for a series of rejuvenation sessions with live-cell applications (the cells come from calf embryos); others have their facial muscles stimulated by a small penlike electrical apparatus called an Excito-moteur; Carita features a gentle, effective "peeling" with a black, gritty product called Rénovateur; up the *rue* at Ingrid Millet one can be treated with a mask made from fresh pineapples; across the Seine, Béatrice Braun *esthéticiennes* will apply collagens and elastins to rejuvenate saggy connective tissue; and at Clarins women pay regular visits to have their skin smoothed with oil extracted from blue orchids.

We may all be born with perfect, poreless skin, but as we grow up, foods, pollution, hormonal changes, sun and assorted bad habits take their toll in lines, wrinkles, large pores, discoloration and skin eruptions which leave tiny scars. In order to keep your skin as smooth and unblemished as possible, it is essential to care for it like the precious substance it is, cleaning it immaculately, shunning heavy doses of sun

The Paris houses offer a wide range of treatments to keep skin clean, healthy and young.

and avoiding harsh products. The French woman is extremely skin conscious; in her beauty routine, facial care has top priority. In the salons and *instituts*, skin care treatments make up the major portion of business.

The basic Paris facial differs a bit from place to place around town. Each salon or *institut de beauté* is unique, with its own special techniques and products. At Carita, where I had my first Paris facial, *esthéticienne* Clementine began my *traitement du visage* by applying makeup remover and wiping it off with cotton and cold water, the standard first step in most facials. Next she sprayed my face with a fine mist of mineral water, and then proceeded to the Rénovateur, gently rubbing the substance all over my face and neck for almost twenty minutes. It burned slightly, stung some, and I was sure that afterwards my face would be red and blotchy. After the Rénovateur treatment came Huile 14, a simple, light vegetable oil to open the pores during the steam treatment that followed. I lay back in a large reclining armchair called a *fauteuil*, while a steam machine, which directs a warm stream of vapor onto the skin, was brought to me. After ten minutes of steaming came the extraction of blackheads and the clearing of blocked pores, followed by a treatment with the Relaxonde. This is a machine with two interchangeable, gently vibrating tips, a large one to stimulate circulation and a smaller one to smooth wrinkles and tired areas of the face, around the nose and mouth and between the eyebrows. Finally came a mask to close the pores, which Clementine removed after ten minutes, with cotton and cold water. When I inspected the results in the mirror, I was amazed to see that there was no redness at all. My skin was smooth and pale, and felt almost like satin.

The treatment facial I had at the Institut Ingrid Millet, where soft sea sounds or chamber music are piped into the cabins, began with a wonderfully soothing massage of the neck and shoulders by *esthéticienne* Marian. This is always done first, *chez* Millet, to relax the client. Then Marian neatened up my eyebrows, plucking away the stray hairs. Ten minutes of a fine mist with a simultaneous facial massage followed. The combined sensation of gentle steam and tranquilizing fingertip massage brought me to the brink of sleep, which, Marian explained, is what a good facial massage should do. After the steam/massage session, Marian took out a tiny vacuum apparatus and proceeded with the deep-pore cleaning. (This was a much more pleasant experience than the deep-pore cleaning in salons where the facialists squeeze the skin manually). Next Marian whisked a small glass bulb, charged with ultraviolet rays and emitting a crackling sound, over my skin to calm and "heal" it. Then came the sea-mud mask (made from a deep-green mud found beneath the Mediterranean, off the coast of Perpignan). The mud, Marian told me, had antibiotic elements also used in medicines. A wet cloth was placed over the mask to keep it moist. After ten minutes the mask was removed and my face sprayed with simulated seawater.

At this point, if you choose, you can have the application of live cells, a rejuvenating treatment. The cells, from a calf embryo, are in a freeze-dried state, and all the *esthéticienne* has to do to bring them back to life is add water. When wet, the cells have a slightly gamy smell, like old meat, but as soon as they are absorbed by the skin (in twenty to thirty seconds) the smell disappears. (As I skeptically listened to Marian explain the treatment, I had visions of these healthy, aggressive, "vital" cells zooming down through my pores to come to the aid of my own poor, overworked cells, close to exhaustion from the effort of keeping my face from falling

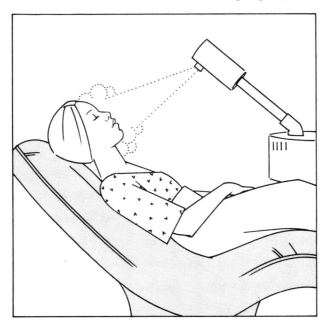

below my chin. I must admit, though, that my skin *did* have an unusual, translucent glow after the application.) The final step of the Ingrid Millet facial is the application of a light, protective cream. After the facial, while you are still reclining, utterly relaxed, in the big armchair of your private cabin, Marian serves you a tray with your choice of tea with honey or coffee. A very classy touch.

The facial in the lovely blue and white cabins of Guerlain concentrated on massage, and included one unusual feature: toward the end of the treatment, *esthéticienne* Aline smoothed on a warm mask which never dried or hardened. It was applied, after the deep pore cleaning, over a special cream that calmed the skin and closed the pores. Aline told me that for fragile skin (which she told me I had), a mask that tightens and dries can be damaging. The warm mask over the cream simply serves to make the cream penetrate more effectively. After the mask was removed, my face was sprayed with icy, aromatic water from an apparatus resembling a small fire extinguisher. Following the facial, you can have a complimentary makeup if you wish, with advice on how to use Guerlain cosmetics. As you leave the salon, a deferential attendant asks if you would like to be sprayed with a Guerlain fragrance and, if you do, proceeds to envelop you in a layer of heavenly scent.

At the Béatrice Braun Institut, I found one of the final steps of a generally very pleasing facial rather odd; this was the use of a machine called an Excito-moteur. Said my *esthéticienne*, Lisa, after she removed the mask, "Now we do gymnastics for your face." She took out a small chrome apparatus which, I soon learned, gives a tiny electric jolt to the individual facial muscles. What it feels like is a muscle twitch. It is supposed to be restorative for faces which have begun to fall—actually any face over the age of twenty-five, although the treatment is most popular with women over fifty. (It is possible to have an Excito-moteur treatment without a facial.) I was told that the apparatus stimulates and firms the muscles of the face, just as regular exercise stimulates, firms and tones the muscles of the body. The method is very similar to facial rehabilitation techniques used for muscles damaged by accident or illness. As the Excito-moteur was being worked over my face, I began to worry: What if one of these muscles gets started and then never stops?

What if the twitch is turned on and Lisa can't turn it off? It didn't happen, and I was told that it doesn't, just as it doesn't happen when you move your own muscles. I wasn't reassured. I only had one treatment, and am still a little young to see a difference. The Excito-moteur was developed for the older woman, and should be taken in a series of eight or ten treatments for noticeable results. Aside from the Excito-moteur, the facial at Béatrice Braun's was extremely soothing, as was the decor of the *institut*, and Madame Braun herself.

Before we proceed with the how-to's of skin care *à la française* there is one important thing I must emphasize: *there are no shortcuts to healthy, beautiful, young-looking skin*. "Anything advertised as an instant treatment has to be false," says Ingrid Millet, "and is probably dangerous. Nature works very slowly. You age slowly, you improve slowly."

You must establish a routine and stick with it. The byword of your beauty-care program should be "regularity." Almost every treatment mentioned in this book, done in a salon or to be done at home, should be scheduled at regular intervals over an extended period of time. This is the bottom line, the key to being *une femme soignée*.

Cleaning Your Skin the French Way

The French woman's skin-care program differs from ours in one fundamental way: she doesn't use soap and water on her face. Instead, she cleans her face with cleansing lotion or cream, followed by a toning or astringent lotion. The French believe that almost any soap is too harsh for the face. Coupled with this, the tap water, particularly in Paris, is very hard, and it tends to dry the skin. (If she does use water on her face, it is usually mineral water from a bottle or a spray.)

Since most of the Parisiennes I saw had fine complexions, I decided to try out their method. My skin reacted so well that I have adopted the following program, set down by Ingrid Millet, permanently. It works well for any skin type, since you buy the necessary products specially formulated for your own skin type—dry, normal, mixed, oily. But this regimen is *particularly* good if you have dry skin.

A Basic
Skin-Care Program

What you need:

- A creamy makeup remover or cleansing lotion
- An alcohol-free toning or astringent lotion, according to skin type
- A stimulating, toning, drying, or moisturizing mask, according to skin type
- A light moisturizer
- Cotton balls

What you do:

Evening

1. Apply the cleansing lotion to your face and neck, smoothing it on with the tips of your fingers in circular movements, starting at your chin and rising to your temples, then from your collarbone to your jaw. This not only helps clean your skin deep down, it acts as a short, stimulating massage, too.

2. Remove the cream with damp cotton balls, wiping upward with long, fluid strokes. (For those of you who do not feel washed unless you rinse your face with water, there are cleansing milks made to be rinsed off with water. Use one of these, or if you prefer to use one of the traditional cleansers, splash your face with water and pat dry after you've removed the cleanser, but before you put on the toner.)

3. Apply the toning lotion to your skin with cotton balls. Continue to wipe with fresh cotton and lotion until every trace of dirt has disappeared.

4. Apply a light, moisturing cream to your face and neck. (Do not use a heavy night cream when you retire. The skin has to breathe at night. A light moisturizer allows skin respiration while keeping the top layer of skin soft, and thus more wrinkle-resistant.) Always apply moisturizer when the skin is still slightly damp, to seal in moisture and lubricate the skin more effectively.

Morning

1. Clean your face with cotton balls saturated with the toning lotion. (Later on, once or twice during the day, give your face a quick, once-over cleaning, just using cotton balls and toning lotion.)

2. To protect your face and neck, apply a moisturizing cream before you go out.

Weekly

To complement your daily cleansing program, Ingrid Millet suggests that you use a mask, formulated for your skin type, once or twice a week. (If you live in an urban area, or have oily skin, you should use a mask twice a week.) Masks deep-clean the skin, tighten the pores, remove dead skin and brighten the complexion. There are moisturizing masks for dry skin and drying masks for oily skin. There are stimulating masks for sluggish skin and toning masks for sagging skin. There are peel-off masks, rinse-off masks and rub-off masks. Ask your facialist or the representative behind the cosmetics counter about the best mask for your skin.

Monthly

Have a salon facial, or do one at home (see later in this chapter).

Exotic Natural Masks to Make

At the Institut Ingrid Millet, two of the popular treatments are the wheat-germ mask and the pineapple mask. You can adapt both of these preparations for home use.

Wheat-Germ Mask: For this mask, which smooths and softens the skin, you will need wheat-germ *powder*, not ordinary, granular wheat germ. The powder, which looks like brown flour, is available at health food stores. (If you cannot find wheat-germ powder, use whole-wheat flour.) Mix half a cup of wheat-germ powder with enough water to make it into a thin paste. Spread the paste onto your face and neck, let dry (about ten minutes), rub off and rinse.

Pineapple Mask: When fresh pineapples are in season, try this refreshing mask, good for all skin types. The natural enzymes in pineapple help remove dead surface cells and clarify the complexion. Cut a large slice of pineapple (peeled and cored) and whip it to a pulp in a blender or mash it finely with a fork. Drain off excess juice. Now apply the pulp to your face. Since this could be a little messy, it's better if you're in a semi-reclining position in a chair or on a bed, with a towel under your head. After fifteen minutes, rinse off.

Protecting Your Skin

Nobody has yet discovered a way to prevent the skin's aging, although millions of dollars are spent every year on research. What you *can* do, though, suggests Béatrice Braun, until the anti-aging pill or cream comes along, is to protect your skin from the external elements that harm it—the sun, wind and pollution. On your own body you can see the difference between the skin that has been the most protected from the elements—on the inside of your upper arm, on your stomach, at the base of your spine—and the skin that has been most exposed—your hands. There may well be twenty years' difference in the appearance of your

skin from one area to the other. The sun destroys delicate connective fibers and thickens the skin, making it less elastic and more wrinkle-prone—damage that is irreparable. You can keep years off your face simply by protecting it with a moisturizer and a sun block. In addition, counsels Madame Braun, who stringently follows her own advice, avoid the products that can damage your skin from the inside—alcohol, refined sugar, starches, coffee and cigarettes (studies have shown that the skin of women who are steady smokers wrinkles earlier than the skin of women who are nonsmokers).

Carita's Skin-Care Tips

Madame Dulac, who has been with the house of Carita for nineteen years, is a small, round, smiling woman responsible for developing all of the Carita skin-care products. She also supervises the Carita *estheticiennes* school, as well as the product export division. Four fundamental, but important, points to remember in caring for your skin are stressed by Madame Dulac, one of the most respected skin-care experts in Paris:

• It is restating the obvious, but the cardinal rule is to always keep your skin clean. Clean your face in the morning, during the day, in the evening before putting on fresh makeup and at night right before you go to bed. (Madame Dulac told me I would be shocked at the number of women who go to bed without removing their makeup. I couldn't tell her that occasionally I was one of that guilty number. But not any more!)

• When you put on or remove lotions or cream, never rub your skin back and forth in ZZZZZZZ's. Apply creams in long, fluid strokes, moving upward, against gravity.

• When cleaning, or applying lotion or cream around the eye area, hold the skin at the outside corner of the eye and, with gentle strokes, wipe inward toward the bridge of the nose. Do this both above and below the eye socket. (Going in the other direction tends to crease the skin around the eyes.)

• Never put heavy creams around your eyes at night. A heavy cream suffocates the skin and makes the eye area swell by morning. Instead, use a very light moisturizer that is quickly absorbed into the skin.

An Herbal Facial Lotion

The Herbier de Provence is a small, charming, and absolutely intoxicating boutique in the heart of the old Les Halles market area, which today is developing into a Soho-like district with small shops and galleries, late-night clubs and inexpensive eating places. The Herbier de Provence, at 19 rue du Jour, dispenses herbs and spices from huge open baskets, which accounts for the fabulous aroma in the air as you enter the shop—almost a "cure" in itself. Along with the herbs, which come mainly, as the sign says, from Provence, you get advice on how to use them from the pleasant, knowledgable shopkeepers.

All over Paris, in the best salons and *instituts*, there is a shift back to natural products. Creams, lotions, masks and oils are being made from fruits, flowers, animal products, vegetables and herbs. In line with this back-to-nature trend, here, from the Herbier de Provence, is a 100 percent natural, revitalizing and toning facial lotion to concoct yourself, good for any type of skin.

What you need:

- One quart water, bottled if possible (the purer the better)
- Four tablespoons 90 percent alcohol (available at a pharmacy)
- Four tablespoons sage
- One tablespoon mint
- One tablespoon basil
- One tablespoon camomile flower tea
- One tablespoon rosemary
  Optional, but recommended if you can find them:
- One tablespoon dried rose petals
- One tablespoon lavender
- One tablespoon linden tea

What you do:

Mix all herbs and flowers with the water. Bring to a boil and let boil for five minutes. Cool and then filter through cheesecloth or a paper coffee filter. Add the alcohol (used to conserve the lotion) and mix. Pour the mixture into a bottle with a fitted cap and keep in a cool place. Use morning and evening, after cleansing, as well as any time during the day to freshen up.

Giving Yourself
A Facial

Doing a facial at home cannot duplicate the experience of having it done professionally. However, if it's not convenient for you to go to a salon, you should incorporate a do-it-yourself facial into your beauty schedule once a month, to clean the skin deep down, and refresh the complexion.

At his modern, flower-filled Centre de Beauté et de Stylisme, located at 71 avenue Marceau, Jean-Pierre Fleurimon teaches his clients how to care for their skin. M. Fleurimon, who also runs a school for *esthéticiennes* and lectures widely, suggests the following simple program for doing a facial at home.

What you need:

- Cleansing lotion
- Cotton balls
- Boiling water
- Facial tissues
- Plain yogurt or commercially prepared calming or healing mask
- A large towel
- Cold water in a small spray bottle or mister
- Moisturizer

What you do:

1. Clean your face thoroughly with the cleansing lotion, massaging the lotion on your skin for five minutes, then removing it with cotton balls.

2. Now you steam your face. To do this, take a pot of boiling water and place it on a trivet or hot plate on a low table. Sitting in front of the steaming pot, take a large towel and make a "tent" over your head, holding the edge of the towel about six inches in front of your forehead. Lean over the pot, but STAY AT LEAST ONE FOOT AWAY. If you get too close, you can burn your skin badly. After ten minutes, pat your face dry.

3. Most skin-care advice you read tells you not to squeeze blackheads. Jean-Pierre Fleurimon says that that is fine advice, but everybody ignores it, since it's almost impossible to resist squeezing a blackhead once you notice one on your skin. M. Fleurimon condones the practice, but only if you make sure your hands are very clean and you do it very gently, with tissues covering the fingers you're using.

At this point in the facial, take a large magnifying mirror and, under a good light, check your face over for blackheads. If you find any, squeeze them very gently between the forefingers of each hand. If you cannot remove them easily, do not squeeze any harder. You could injure your skin by breaking tiny capillaries.

4. Apply a calming mask, or use plain yogurt—one of the most soothing natural products around—as a mask. After ten minutes, remove the mask with damp cotton balls.

5. Spray your face all over with a fine mist of icy water, scented if you wish with rose water or a drop of cologne. Gently pat your skin dry. Apply a light moisturizer around your eyes.

6. If at all possible, do not apply makeup for several hours after your facial. Let your skin breathe. Jean-Pierre Fleurimon suggests that the best time to do a facial is in the evening before you go to bed.

Under-Eye Treatments

The under-eye area is one of the first places on your face to show age. There the skin is thin and delicate, and the muscles underneath are in motion with every expression, every blink you make. Tear ducts and sinuses also affect this fragile section of your face. When you care for the under-eye area, you must use extreme attention and a light hand.

Béatrice Braun Under-Eye Massage

This is a little exercise in face maintenance that you should start practicing now and continue forever. It will help prevent the development of under-eye "bags" by decongesting the area of water and fatty deposits.

With the pads of your two index fingers, press firmly for five seconds against the bridge of your nose, next to the inside corners of your eyes. Then move your fingers slightly down, to the edge of the bone of the eye socket, and press here for five seconds. Continue moving your fingers outward along the eye socket, pressing slowly and firmly, for five seconds at each point, beyond the temples, all the way to the hairline. This procedure should be done every evening after you clean your face and are ready for bed.

Masque Glacé Isabelle Lancray

The Lancray Institut has a popular treatment for tired, puffy eyes, called a *masque glacé*. This is an actual mask, Lone Ranger style, made out of clear plastic and filled with a gelatinlike product that does not harden. (Some U.S. pharmacies carry similar masks, one brand called "Looky," one called "Masque de Gelé.") The mask is placed in a freezer for an hour or two, then applied to the eye area for about fifteen minutes. You can adapt this treatment by folding a washcloth or small linen hand towel into a small rectangle to cover the eye area, dipping into a bowl of ice water until it is completely soaked, squeezing off the excess water, and then applying it to your eyes as you recline. Rewet the cloth once or twice as it warms up. This treatment reduces swelling and stimulates circulation in the eye area. It is not recommended if you have sinus trouble.

Maintaining a Firm, Youthful Neck and Jaw

Exposed to the same elements as the face, the neck often does not get the same care. Without the benefits of cleansing and moisturizing, the neck ages faster, eventually appearing older than the face above it. A sagging jawline can also betray age. Madame Perrine Pultz, *directrice* of the Institut Isabelle Lancray, says that with conscientious care and a simple exercise, your neck and jaw will complement and not detract from your face.

If you were to go to the Lancray Institut, you would be treated with an apparatus that electrically stimulates your facial, jaw and neck muscles. But since this method is only available in the salon, Madame Pultz prescribes a minicare program for her clients, and for you, to do at home:

1. After cleaning your face *and neck* with cleansing and toning lotions, do this little exercise for firming the neck and jawline: Looking in the mirror, make a forced, exaggerated smile (without clenching your teeth), tensing all the muscles of your neck and jaw as though you were making an "eeeeeeeeeeee" sound. Now relax. Tense and relax repeatedly for one minute.

2. With your chin raised, apply a moisturizing cream to the neck by alternating both hands in a gentle, downward motion, one hand after the other, starting at the jawbone and descending below the collarbone. Repeat this delicate massage until all the cream has been absorbed.

55

Most of the Parisiennes I saw had fine complexions.

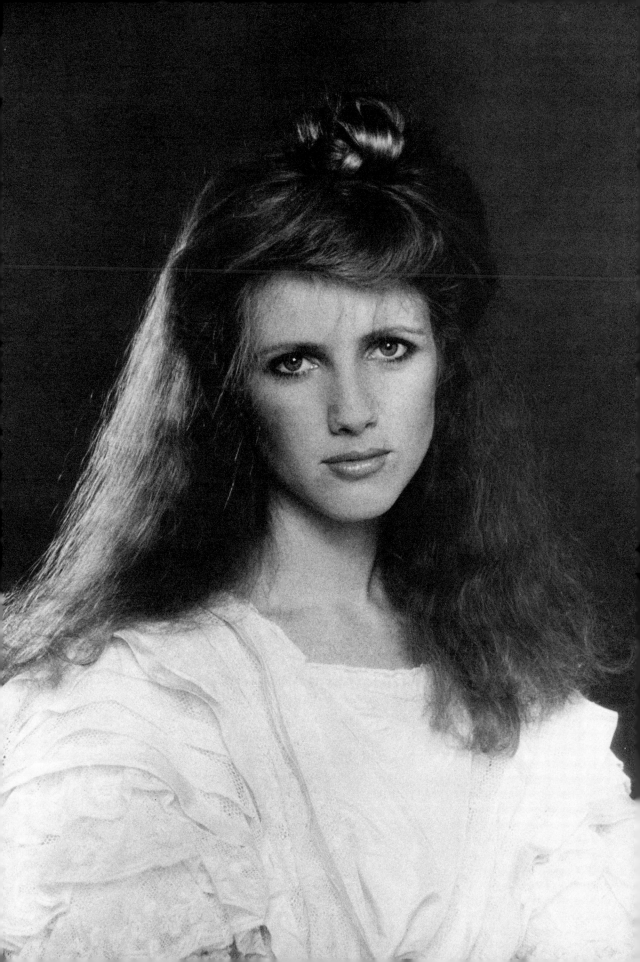

Complexion Pickup

There is a pill called Bronz-Activ, not yet available in the U.S., that was becoming a crazy success while I was in Paris. This pill, which is essentially concentrated carrot juice—carotene—was turning chic Parisians a sort of orangey-brown, giving them the appearance of having a slightly faded tan, the look of someone who had come back from the Caribbean a week and a half ago. The only problem with it was that if you took a few more pills than the recommended dose, in an effort to deepen your "tan," the palms of your hands and the soles of your feet would turn bright orange. Despite this drawback, the pill has made the young doctor who conceived the idea a millionaire.

If you feel particularly grey after a bout with the flu or from a general malaise, here's a tasty "cure" from Béatrice Braun that will have your face glowing within a month. It's a simple variation of the Bronz-Activ idea, but it won't turn your palms or soles orange. Every morning for four to six weeks, drink a glass of carrot juice spiked with a generous squeeze of lemon juice. You'll have the healthiest-looking face on your block!

The Most Essential Beauty Product

In spite of all the superb cosmetic products available today, water, says Ingrid Millet, is the most essential beauty product of all. French women drink a great deal of water, both mineral and tap variety—often two quarts a day in addition to anything else they drink. Water keeps your system clean, aids digestion and elimination and acts as an internal moisturizer for your skin. Madame Millet drinks a large glass of room-temperature water as soon as she gets up in the morning. It's as much a part of her daily routine as brushing her teeth.

Some French women, particularly those who work in offices or who travel often in airplanes (where the air is super-dry), carry a small atomizer of water with them and spray their faces with a fine mist three or four times a day. We might be wise to adopt this practice. The central heating in our offices and apartments is very drying for the skin (as well as for the nasal and throat passages). Spray cans of Évian mineral water, available in some U.S. pharmacies and department stores, are perfect to use because the water is pure and the spray is extremely fine. If you can't find these spray cans, buy a very small plant mister and refill it every day with bottled or tap water. Keep the mister or spray can with you in a tote bag or on your desk. Several times a day, give your face a light misting, right over your makeup. Moisturizing from within and without is one of the best ways to keep your skin young and fresh.

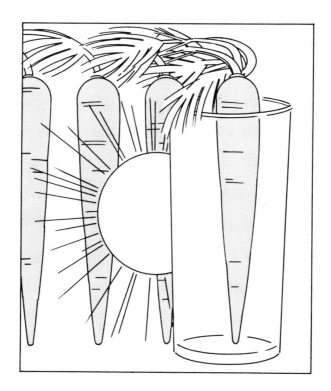

III
YOUR MAKEUP

Makeup in Paris is at once subtle and dramatic. The women appear fresh-faced, but with a certain intensity to their look. While observing French women in a fashionable café, and trying to analyze exactly what their special style was, I noticed that most of them seemed to emphasize their eyes dramatically and play down their mouths. Later I asked Thibault, the sought-after makeup artist at Carita, about this technique. "Of course," he said, "that's natural. You emphasize *either* your eyes *or* your mouth. But never both. Otherwise, you'll look like a gypsy."

The trend in Paris makeup for daytime is toward the soft, understated and romantically feminine. For evening the look is more intense, glamorous, but never heavy-handed. Styles have changed markedly since 1767, when Benjamin Franklin wrote a letter to a friend, describing the fashion in Paris makeup:

As to Rouge, they don't pretend to imitate nature in laying it on. . . . I have not had the honour of being at any Lady's Toylette, but I fancy I can tell you how it is done; cut a Hole of 3 inches in diameter (in a piece of paper) in such a manner as the top of the Hole may be placed just under your eye; then, with a brush dipped in colour, paint Face and Paper together; when the Paper is taken off there will remain a Patch of Red

exactly the form of the Hole. This is the Mode, from Actresses on the Stage thro all Ranks of Ladies.

Today, bright reds, greens, oranges and blues are out (except with Saint Laurent, whose makeup collection, running against the tide, features some brilliant blues, reds and yellows to match the colors of his fabrics). In general, dusty, muted colors—rose, teal blue, ocher, moss—are favored, with neutrals—gradations of greys and browns—shadowing the eyes.

The key word with almost all the makeup experts I interviewed was "harmony"—harmony of color and tone between your eyeshadow, blusher, foundation and lipstick, harmony between your makeup and your clothes.

Thibault, who is the preferred *visagiste* (face expert) of Catherine Deneuve, favors a delicate, natural look, the face fresh and luminescent. The texture of his makeups is transparent and silky, with the skin underneath always visible. "Makeup should serve to exteriorize and enhance the personality of a woman," says Thibault, "be it adventurous and theatrical, or earthy and natural. Every woman has her own unique style, and her makeup should reflect it."

For Jacques Clemente, an extraordinary makeup artist whose strapping, powerful build belies his artistic cosmetic trade, the goal of makeup is to accentuate the positive facial features. "To this end," says M. Clemente, who is the resident artist for Elizabeth Arden in Paris, "you must know your face—your skin, your bones, your features. Study your face in front of a three-way mirror. Like a sculptor, gently press your fingers against the bones and follow them; feel the muscles of your facial structure; trace the lines of your face—around the chin and jaw, the cheekbones and the forehead. To apply makeup well, you must be completely familiar with the anatomy of your face."

When you are made up in a Paris salon, you lie back in a large, reclining *fauteuil* (armchair), situated in the middle of a small, brilliantly lit cabin. The makeup artist works over you almost in the posture of a dentist, choosing products and implements from a well-stocked cart or countertop. You rarely get to observe the "work in progress," the artist preferring that you not look until he has applied the finishing touch. It was always a slight shock for me to see myself exquisitely and professionally made up, having last viewed my image barefaced.

A *maquillage* (makeup) is usually an hour-long process, beginning with the removal of your old makeup and the tweezing of your eyebrows. During this early stage, the makeup artist will ask what kind of occasion you are going to attend and what you plan to wear, so that he can design a makeup accordingly. Then the foundation base is applied, followed by translucent powder to "set" it. The most time-consuming part of a *maquillage* is the eyes, which can take forty-five minutes or more to complete. Eyes are highlighted, contoured, shadowed, lined, powdered and mascara'd, using a plethora of brushes, colors and products. Results can be extraordinary. Afterwards, contour powder, blusher and highlighter are applied to your cheeks, chin and forehead. Finally, the lips are carefully outlined and lipstick is brushed on. *Voilà!* You are allowed to sit up and gaze at your finished face.

After talking with and being "transformed" by the finest *visagistes* in Paris, I came to realize that, once you master the fundamental skills, everything is possible and acceptable in makeup. Your makeup kit is your palette, your face the canvas. You can employ a wide range of techniques and cover the canvas with color, being as audacious and inventive as you want; or you can leave the canvas bare, save for an artfully applied brushstroke or two. The only imperative is that you feel comfortable in your face.

RECIPE FOR A BASIC MAKEUP

Olivier Echaudemaison is a young, self-assured makeup artist who works with the Harriet Hubbard Ayer Salon, often in tandem with master hairstylist Alexandre. He seems to have the royal touch, since he is often requested by Princess Anne of England, as well as by the Princesses Grace and Caroline of Monaco, to design and apply their makeup for special occasions.

"Makeup is a game," says Olivier. "To learn how to do it well, you must start slowly and learn the basic elements, just as with tennis, chess, skiing or bridge. Another parallel would be with cooking. When you are learning, you start simply, without mixing too many ingredients."

Here is Olivier's recipe for a basic makeup (see illustration in color section):

What you need:

- A light, airy foundation base, matched as closely as possible to the skin tone of your neck
- Translucent powder
- A fluffy cosmetic puff or large, soft brush
- Two eye shadows: a neutral, dark-grey or brown shadow and a lighter shade such as pink or beige
- Black or brown mascara
- Lipstick
- Lip gloss (optional)

"There are no more set rules for fashion and beauty," Jacques Clemente told me. "Think of styles—in fashion, hair and makeup—as suggestions, not directives. Take from the current trends what suits you. As in a laboratory, you take a little of this, a little of that, put it together and see if it works."

What you do:

1. After your face is perfectly clean, and you've applied a light moisturizer to your face and neck, smooth on the foundation base. Remember to graduate the makeup base down to your throat, so that there is no obvious line of demarcation between your chin and neck.

2. Brush your face lightly with translucent powder to set the base.

3. Apply the dark, neutral eye shadow to your eyelid, and then the lighter shade from the top of your eyelid (where the brow bone starts) to your eyebrow. As you apply the eye shadows, look at yourself in profile in the mirror. The line of the eye makeup should always go up, never down. Blend the line between the two shadows well, so that it is not obvious where one stops and the other begins.

4. Apply two coats of mascara to your upper and lower lashes, removing any smudges with a Q-tip and a tiny bit of cream.

5. Your lipstick should be in harmony with your shadow. If you use a green or brown shadow, your lipstick should be in the orange/brown family. If your shadow is lavender, blue or grey, then your lipstick should be in the blue family—that is, plum, rose or pink. If you use a dark lipstick, apply a translucent gloss over it so that it doesn't look heavy or thick. A woman should have several lipsticks, at least four or five, to go with her outfits, suggests Olivier. It's a small, inexpensive accessory, and the right one can make a big difference in your look.

Makeup in Paris is at once subtle and dramatic.

How to Achieve Harmony

When your makeup is as mellow as a major chord, with all the elements in harmony, your face will have a neat, fine, finished look. Thibault, of Carita, has illustrated two examples of harmonized makeup—a gold-toned face and a rose-toned face—which are illustrated in the color section. For Thibault, the gold-toned face is more of a daytime look, because the colors are warm and sunny. The rose-toned face is an evening look, with its colors cool as moonlight. Try these two harmonized looks on yourself. The list of what you need for each makeup can be found accompanying the illustrations. Remember to key these makeups to your outfit if you are going out—the gold-toned face for clothes in the beige/brown/gold/yellow/orange/green family, the rose-toned face for clothes in the blue/grey/burgundy/purple/rose family.

Using Blusher to Your Best Advantage

Terry, another talented young makeup artist at Carita, offers some tips on how to use blusher correctly.

- When you use liquid, cream or gel blush, apply it directly after the foundation, before you brush with translucent powder. With a powder blush, apply with a big, soft brush after you've brushed on the powder, touching your cheeks very lightly.
- If you have a long face, apply the blush straight across your cheekbones to the temples. This makes the face look wider. And add a touch of blush on the chin. This tends to shorten a long face.
- For a round face, apply blush in long strokes, under the cheekbones to the temples.

- To emphasize the eyes, apply the blush high up on your cheeks, just under the eyes, and extend it around and out to the temples.
- For a healthy, "kissed by the sun" look, put blush high on your cheeks and extend it over the bridge of your nose, just the way the sun would tan you. Then put dabs high on your forehead and chin. For this technique to work, blush must be lightly applied and very well blended so that the color looks completely natural.

Making the Most of Your Mouth

Thibault explains how to subtly accentuate your mouth: With a lip pencil in either a warm brown or the same color as your lipstick, lightly outline the edge of your lips. Then smooth the outline over with your fingertips so that it barely shows. Now apply lipstick to the outer half of your lips. Fill in lips with a slightly lighter shade of lipstick in the same tone. If you are going out at night, apply a small dab of colorless gloss. For daytime, lipstick should be matte. (If you do emphasize your mouth, keep your eyes understated and neutral, with a little grey or brown shadow and mascara.)

On Contouring

Did you think Catherine Deneuve had a perfect, oval face? I did, but I learned from Thibault that she's not quite as perfect as she looks. She has a square face corrected by blusher and contour powder, shadowed under her cheeks and chin.

Contouring is a rather advanced makeup technique, where you shadow those features you want to de-emphasize in order to camouflage facial faults, or to accentuate a feature by shadowing around it. The best way to learn how to do it is to buy brown contour powder or brown blusher and practice in front of a well-lit mirror.

Here are some basic techniques:

- To narrow a wide nose, shadow along the sides of the nose from the bridge to the nostrils.
- To shorten a long nose, shadow under the tip of the nose.
- To soften a large jaw and give an illusion of ovalness to the face, shadow under the chin and jawbone.
- To emphasize cheekbones, shadow under the bones, extending the powder to the temples.
- To emphasize or give the illusion of a cleft chin, put a touch of contour powder at the bottom of your chin in the center. (This trick is used mainly for photographs.)
- To narrow a wide forehead, shadow the sides of the forehead above the temples.
- To widen a narrow forehead, shadow two small areas above each eyebrow.
- To emphasize your eyes, use the powder to shadow the area under your brow bone, extending out to the temple.

Remember, contour powder must be *perfectly* blended so that it truly looks like shadow and not makeup.

All Eyes

Your eyes are your most striking facial feature, sparkling jewels that demand a beautiful setting. The French woman makes up her eyes with great care, accentuating them to their best advantage. She tends to use more eyeliner or crayon on the upper and lower lids, and more mascara on the upper and lower lashes. She lines the inside of the lower lid with black, grey or blue pencil, and extends the eyeshadow below the brow bone almost to the end of the eyebrow, giving the eyes intensity and width. In the illustration in the color section, you will find a French-style eye to try yourself, designed from my own observations.

On Mascara

Mascara, according to Thibault, is your one most essential makeup item. It's more important than shadow, because it gives an intensity to your look that shadow doesn't. If you have only one thing to put on, make it mascara.

When applying mascara, you'll get the best results if you powder your lashes before and after the first coat. Many women, when patting on the translucent powder over their foundation base, simply include their eyelashes at the same time. To avoid clumps of mascara, brush your lashes, between the first and second coat, with a tiny lash brush or old toothbrush, to separate them. For really dramatic, "Hollywood" lashes, do what the makeup artists do: curl your lashes first with an eyelash curler, then apply mascara in cake form with a brush. The "old-fashioned" mascara gives you complete control over the consistency and amount of mascara you apply, because you add water to the dry mascara and mix it yourself.

Here's a super-practical tip for removing mascara, offered by José Luis, the delightful Chilean makeup artist for Yves Saint Laurent. To take your mascara off at night without smearing it all over your eyes and face, you will need a spoon, baby oil (or makeup-removing oil) and a tissue. Wrap the tissue around your forefinger and pour several drops of oil onto it. Then take the spoon and place your thumb in the bowl of the spoon, curved side out. Now take several lashes at a time between the spoon and the tissue, starting at the base of the lash, and *very gently* remove the mascara by sliding the lashes between your fingers from the base to the tips.

The Best Colors for Your Eyes

To play up your eyes, you should choose the colors of your shadows to complement or contrast with the color of your eyes. Terry, from Carita, offers some general suggestions on shadows that will bring out the best in brown, blue and green eyes.

Brown Eyes: Use warm, brown shadows (chestnut or golden brown), mossy greens or greys. A slightly gold-tinged shadow will bring out the warmth and light in brown eyes. Use black mascara.

*Blue Eyes***:** Do *not* use a blue shadow the same color, or brighter, than your eyes. This tends to make your eye color look washed out. Rather, you should use shades of grey-blue, cinnamon or, for evening, a mix of grey and mauve. Use black or midnight-blue mascara.

Green Eyes: Do *not* use a green shadow the same color as or lighter than your eyes. Instead, for contrast, use a cinnamon or chocolate-toned shadow, or dark green, or grey-green. Outline your eyes with brown pencil to intensify your look. Use black or brown mascara.

Mixing and Matching Shadows

Once you have mastered the basics, you can start to mix several shadows to add depth and interest to your eyes. On the eyelid, suggests Olivier Echaudemaison, the colors can be graduated, darker on the outside of the lid, lighter on the inside, near the nose. (Never the other way around.) For example, you can put a soft brown shadow on the outside of the lid, a rosy beige on the inside. Or you can put lavender on the outside and pink on the inside. Then, depending on the colors on the lid, you can put a third shadow—a dark, neutral grey or brown—on the brow bone, extending to the outer tip of the eyebrow, almost to the temple, and a fourth shadow—a pale, complementary beige or pink— directly under the eyebrow. All shadows must be very well blended. You can do this with all kinds of color combinations; greens and greys, greens and blues, blues and greys, pinks and blues, browns and corals, lavender and apricot, or browns and greys. Play with your palette and use your imagination.

To Make Your Eyes Look Larger

If your eyes are small or inset, or if you just want to make your eyes look huge, Jacques Clemente reveals this simple technique: With a white eye pencil or crayon, put a dot of color at the outside corner of each eye and blend. Then line the inside of the lower lids with the white crayon. Now apply the rest of your eye makeup. Use a pale shadow, or shadows, on the lid.

Strange and Striking

For an unusual evening look (and it is *very* unusual), try this technique from Jacques Clemente: Use no blusher at all on your cheekbones. Instead, put the blush all around your eyes, as shadow on the lids, as well as under the lower lids, above the eyebrows and at the temples.

For daytime, José Luis prefers simplicity in makeup.

Erasing Circles and Shadows Under Your Eyes

Carita's Terry advises against using a stick cover-up to camouflage under-eye circles and shadows. A stick is too heavy for the delicate under-eye area, and too obvious. Instead, Terry suggests that you use a very light makeup base, several shades lighter than your normal shade. This covers shadows and sets off your eyes to advantage.

A Sheer Daytime Look

José Luis, who designs the makeup for Saint Laurent's twice-yearly haute couture collections, likes lavish, fantastic makeup for evening. But for daytime, he prefers simplicity. "I love the look of the bare eyelid," he says. "It's like the petal of a flower." The only eye makeup he suggests for day is two coats of black or brown mascara, intensified by brown, black or blue crayon dotted among the lashes. If you want a daytime look that's a little more special, apply just a touch of shadow the same color as your outfit, under the outer arch of your eyebrow.

Grooming Your Eyebrows

Paris eyebrows are "liberated"—thicker, and more even in width than before. The look is natural but neat. Skinny, pencil-thin brows are definitely out. So are brows that go from thick to thin. Tweezing eyebrows, the only facial feature you can change at will, is an essential part of every professional makeup session. Here are some tips culled from the experts for tweezing your own eyebrows:

- Eyebrows should generally start on the same vertical line as the inside corner of your eye.
- Leave a few sparse hairs at the beginning of the brows, to emphasize a soft, natural, younger look.
- Before you pluck, dab a cotton ball soaked with warm water on the area. Hair will be easier to remove. Then brush your eyebrows up so you can see the true line of the brow. This facilitates neat, even plucking.
- Always pluck from the inside edge of the brow at the bridge of the nose toward the outside, following the natural line of the brow.

A Progressive Makeup Program

Jacques Clemente, who is almost as well known in Paris for his courtly personality and solicitous care of his clients as he is for his makeup skills, believes that too much makeup early in the day looks tacky and clownish. So he has devised a makeup schedule to keep a woman fresh-faced in the morning, dramatic at night. According to Jacques' plan, which I've dubbed "progressive makeup," you should apply your makeup little by little throughout the day, adding color and definition as the hours grow later and the shadows longer. Here is the Jacques Clemente day-to-night timetable:

9:00 A.M. Apply a light makeup base or tinted moisturizer to your face and throat. Add a touch of cream or liquid blusher. Put clear or tinted lip gloss on your lips, and brush your lashes with brown or black mascara.

Noon. Lightly powder your face with translucent loose powder. With a light hand, brush powdered blusher on your cheekbones. Line the inside of your lower lids with black or dark-brown crayon or pencil. Apply lipstick.

79

6:00 P.M. For evening, you'll probably want to start your makeup from scratch after washing your face. Now you can apply a foundation base and matching or translucent powder if you use them. Then, in addition to putting on the products you used earlier in the day, concentrate on the details that make for an understated evening look: add a deep-toned, earthy eye shadow to your lids; brush several layers of mascara on your upper and lower lashes; over your lipstick, apply a generous amount of gloss; and, finally, add touches of iridescent highlight powder or cream to your forehead, the upper, outer edges of your cheekbones and under your eyes.

Highlighting

Here's a grab bag of Jacques Clemente tips for lighting up your face and décolleté:

- If your hair is very short, or put up to expose your ears, put a tiny dab of blush on each earlobe, and blend.
- For a low-cut dress, smooth a small amount of gold shadow over the curve of the breasts, to catch the light.
- Try a dab of lip gloss, either colorless or tinted, on your cheekbones and under your eyebrow.
- For evening, particularly if your skin looks tired and grey, add a tiny bit or rose color, such as a dot of liquid blusher, to your foundation base. Or, use a base one shade pinker than your daytime shade. This will give your skin a luminescent, healthy glow.

Special Makeup for Special Lighting

If you know ahead of time what kind of lighting you will be seen by, you should make yourself up accordingly, suggests Jean-Pierre Fleurimon. Of course, during the course of a day we are seen by several kinds of light. But there are situations where, most of the time, you are seen by one kind of light more than another: Perhaps you spend eight hours of the day in an office under fluorescent light, or you are giving a small, intimate dinner to be lit by candles. In cases like these, use makeup that the lights will complement. M. Fleurimon gives a popular, four-lesson makeup course at his Centre de Beauté et de Stylisme, in which he covers makeup tips for artificial lights. Here are the basic rules; see the color section for illustrations.

Electric or Incandescent Light tends to wash out color, says M. Fleurimon. Under electric light use bright, clear pinks or reds for lipstick and blusher, true browns or blues for eye shadow. Avoid pale colors, such as soft pink, powder blue or mint green.

Fluorescent Light, the most ghastly illumination around, is a cold light that shows up imperfections and fatigue. To counteract the effects of this light, choose warm colors—coral, mandarin red, tomato—for lipstick and blusher, and gold-frosted shadows for your eyes. Lips should be carefully outlined. Avoid greys, browns and greens.

Candlelight is the most flattering of light embellishing everyone it touches with a romantic glow. To contrast with the golden cast of the flame, use soft, muted, blue-toned colors such as rose, plum, mauve, cherry or lavender. M. Fleurimon recommends you use perhaps a little more blusher than usual to accentuate the contours of your face. Avoid orange-toned lipstick and blusher, as well as dark-grey or brown eye shadows.

Makeup needs are slightly different for women 'of a certain age.'

For Women "Of a Certain Age"

The French are extremely discreet about a woman's age, and for a woman over forty-five or fifty, the classic phrase "a woman of a certain age" is still used. If you are "of a certain age," your makeup needs are slightly different from those of a younger woman. The Paris experts have some tips specifically for you:

- Your makeup should be soft, light and translucent, says Thibault, with very little powder.
- Stay out of the sun as much as possible. A dark tan makes a grey-haired woman look older, and her skin look leathery. Also, after fifty the sun causes the skin to spot.
- Olivier says that your foundation base should be pink-toned, rather than beigey or tan.
- A liquid or gel blusher is more flattering than powder or cream because it gives a softer look.
- Avoid colors that are harsh or bright, both in your makeup and in your clothes.
- Lipstick should never be dark, advises Olivier, in brown or purple tones. Keep lipstick a clear red or a deep pink.
- "Colored shadow on a wrinkled lid is not pretty," Thibault says simply. For the older woman it's often better for the mouth to be bright and well defined, with mascara and just a touch of neutral shadow on the lid.

IV
Your Hair

Just as the proper frame makes an enormous difference to a great painting, your hairstyle makes an enormous difference to your face. A Rubens or a Michelangelo would look as wrong in a sleek chrome frame as a Jackson Pollack encased in gilded baroque wood. The frame must be carefully chosen to complement its subject.

Finding a hairstyle that frames your face to its best advantage will probably involve some trial and error. "You must experiment," says Alexandre. "Pick styles and hair colors that appeal to you and try them out. Don't be rigid and rule-bound about your appearance. In trying new things you may make a few mistakes, but they're worth it to find a look that suits you to perfection."

Paris is a city full to overflowing with hairstyles and ideas offered by her 4,500 hairdressers. At any given moment there must be at least 500 new ways a woman could choose to do her hair, ranging from classic elegance to wild avant-garde. The major trend over the past few years has been toward the shorter, sleeker, sculpted cut, shaped to the head and virtually carefree between cuts. With these cuts, even blow-drying is obsolete. Hair is kept from one to five inches long and cut blunt or layered, according to your face and the contour of your head. Some of these styles are lightly permed for movement, not frizz. After shampooing, you towel-dry, then finger-comb your hair into the shape and waves you want, and let the hair dry by itself.

Paris coiffure is moving away from "done"-looking hair. "Fifteen years ago," explains Jean-Marc Maniatis, probably the most influential young *coiffeur* in Paris today, "women wanted to look coiffed. They went to the hairdresser once or twice a week for sets and comb-outs. And then they were afraid to do anything—go out in the rain, play sports, go to sleep, make love—for fear of ruining their hair. A woman should have a hairstyle that lets her be free, one that looks good after a walk in the wind by the sea. With today's new cuts, the head is liberated. And when the head is liberated, the whole way a woman sees herself changes. She becomes freer, and more truly herself."

The look for daytime may be casual and carefree, but for evening it's elegant and *raffiné*. After the sun goes down, the ever-popular chignon, in one of its myriad forms, is still the preferred *coiffure du soir* for many women. But not the bouffant, fussy updos of yesteryear. Today's chignons (the blanket word that covers any kind of looped, twisted, wrapped or attached hair) create a small, neat head, accessorized with combs, barrettes, ribbon, flowers or any fanciful object or material.

Hair-conditioning treatments, following the Paris back-to-nature trend, are reverting to natural products. The big salons are using plants, herbs and animal proteins to condition problem hair. The Caritas are using placenta concentrates for lifeless hair, oak and walnut bark distillates to fortify fine hair and golden oil from pollen to condition and give shine to dry, fragile hair. Luis Llongueras treats clients with a shampoo containing juniper oil fortified with cinnamon and lemon for oily hair, one with thyme for drab hair and one with eucalyptus for dandruff. And at Maurice Franck you can have a conditioning treatment with fresh algae flown in regularly from Brittany.

All over town there is a new emphasis on maintaining lustrous, beautiful, undamaged hair. In the area of hair coloring, treatments are gentler now, using as few chemicals as possible. Salons are moving away from the radical tranformations that required stripping and recoloring. Instead they are enriching or highlighting what is already there with henna, or a process called *balayage*—a delicate streaking technique that adds light and movement. At-home color treatments are not advised except for the very simplest processes, such as a camomile rinse or lightening a few tiny strands. Chances for long-range damage are high, and results are almost never as good as salon treatments.

Natural Hair-Care Treatments

Cosmetic counters and pharmacy shelves are loaded with commercial preparations to treat every conceivable hair problem. But sometimes natural is better—fewer chemicals, fewer side effects, healthier for you. Here are several hair-care treatments based on natural products, adapted from those used in the Paris salons.

Watercress Treatment for Oily Hair

Clients at the Louis G. Salon swear that this preparation works wonders on oily hair, keeping hair bouncy and oil-free longer. Take a handful of watercress (a plant rich in iron and phosphorus, as well as vitamins A, C and E), and macerate in a blender or food processor with one cup of water. Boil ten minutes, strain out the watercress and cool. Apply the mixture carefully to damp, shampooed hair and leave for twenty minutes. Rinse thoroughly with cold water.

Lemon-Juice Rinse

This is one of the oldest hair treatments around, but it's still one of the best. Louis G. uses a lemon-juice rinse regularly to leave all hair types squeaky clean and shiny. Squeeze and strain the juice of half a lemon into a cup of cold water and stir. Pour over damp hair, leave for three minutes, then rinse with cold water.

Beef-Marrow Treatment for Dry, Damaged Hair

The *moelle de boeuf* (beef-marrow) treatment is currently very big at several Paris salons, including Louis G. and Alexandre. It is used, sometimes fortified with vitamins, before a permanent, after coloring and as a conditioner for dry, damaged, lifeless hair. Beef marrow is rich in natural oils and proteins and gives a beautiful, healthy sheen to problem hair. To give yourself a *moelle de boeuf* treatment, buy three large marrow bones at your butcher, and have him crack them in half. At home, scoop out the marrow, a thick, whitish paste, and, in a small saucepan, mix it with one cup of water, and bring to boil. Let boil down ten minutes, then remove from heat and pour into cup or pyrex dish. (If you have cheesecloth, strain the mixture as you pour.) Cool for about 2 hours. Pure marrow will separate from water and residue and solidify. Work the marrow in your hands to warm it slightly before putting it on. Apply the marrow to dry, unwashed hair with your fingers, one strand at a time, starting at your scalp and woring out to the ends. Leave for half an hour, then shampoo out with mild baby shampoo and rinse with cold water. If your hair is in particularly bad shape, you can make this treatment even more effective by wrapping your head with a hot towel (soaked in hot water, then wrung out). After fifteen minutes, rewet the towel in hot water, wring, and wrap your head for another fifteen minutes. Then shampoo and rinse.

Yeast Cure for Problem Hair

Several French women I met condition their hair from within as well as without. They incorporate nonfermenting brewer's yeast, a natural protein with essential amino acids and rich in B vitamins, into their diets to strengthen and beautify hair and nails. One heaping tablespoon a day, sprinkled on cereal or mixed with yogurt, soup or fruit juice, is all you need to give your diet a healthy supplement of vitamins and protein. Most health food stores have a wide variety of nonfermenting, nutritional yeast to choose from.

Herbal Rinses

Camomile for Blond Hair. This recipe for adding ash-blond lights to light brown or blond hair comes from the Herbier de Provence. Put ten teabags or ten tablespoons of camomile flower tea in one quart of water and boil for ten minutes. Let cool (strain if you use loose tea), then pour over damp, rinsed hair after your shampoo. Do not rinse again. Makes enough for four rinses. Store in the refrigerator.

Thyme Anti-dandruff Rinse: The herb thyme, I was told at the Herbier de Provence, has mild antiseptic properties, and can be effective in

There is a new emphasis on maintaining lustrous, beautiful, undamaged hair.

helping to alleviate dandruff. Boil four heaping tablespoons of thyme in two cups of water for ten minutes. Strain and cool. Pour one cup over damp, shampooed hair, making sure the liquid covers the scalp. Massage in gently. Do not rinse. Makes enough for two treatments.

Rosemary Revitalizing Rinse. The herb rosemary is a stimulant. When your hair looks drab and lifeless, particularly during the winter when it's often kept under wraps, try a rosemary rinse, also from the Herbier de Provence. Prepare it exactly the same way you prepare the thyme rinse, above.

Flouring the Frizzies

The Claude Maxime salon, an ultramodern establishment near the Étoile, with round rooms and polished chrome accents, has a new conditioning treatment concocted from an ancient recipe, using a flour paste for very frizzy hair. This treatment doesn't straighten the hair, but it does smooth down the scales of the hair shaft, making the hair shinier and more manageable. The exact ingredients of the Claude Maxime treatment are secret, but you can make an adaptation of it.

For wild, frizzy/kinky hair, try this: Make a thin, gooey paste (the consistency of cake batter) from a cup of flour and approximately two-thirds cup of cold water. Mix until all lumps have disappeared. Apply this mixture to dry, unwashed hair, smoothing the mixture and your hair straight back. Leave for twenty minutes, then rinse thoroughly under the shower. It will take about five minutes to rinse all the flour out. Now shampoo hair once with baby shampoo or other very mild shampoo. Rinse hair with cool water.

Hair-Setting Gimmicks and Gadgets

Paris salons are usually the first with new ways to work with hair. Here are five unusual hair-setting techniques, none of which uses rollers.

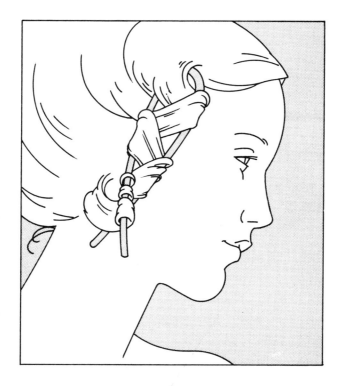

For Face-Framing Waves

This technique for medium-length hair is from *coiffeur* Jacques France. You will need two pieces of heavy coated electrical wire, each about one foot long, available at hardware and electrical supply stores. Bend each piece in half, in the shape of a giant hairpin. After you wash your hair, part it in the middle. When hair is just damp, not wet, take a large strand of hair on one side of the part and, holding the cable about two inches from the part, weave the strand over and under each side of the cable. Attach at the bottom with elastic or string. For a loose wave, wrap about five times; for a tighter wave, eight to ten times. You can also do this with two strands of hair. The rest of your hair can be left natural, or turned under on big rollers at the base of the neck. Let dry and comb lightly.

For a Billowing "Cloud" of Hair

This is called the *tornillon* technique, from Patrick Alès. It creates a full, airy look in medium to long hair. Divide your hair down the center, from your forehead to the base of your neck. Then make another part across your head from one ear to the other. Take the hair from the left front section and twist it around your finger into a tight "rope." Then let this twisted strand recoil naturally, and wind the ends into a small, tight *tornillon*. (The resulting knot looks something like the shell of a snail.) Tuck in the ends and fix with a hairpin. Repeat with the right front section. Now divide the back section into six equal parts, holding each section apart with clips. Twist all six sections into *tornillons*. Let dry and brush out.

For All-over Waves

This technique, also from Patrick Alès, uses sheets of aluminum foil to protect hair from a curling iron and to seal in the wave. On clean, dry hair, divide the top layer of hair into one-inch strands and wrap each strand in a single sheet of aluminum foil, making sure the whole strand is covered, and press flat. Then, with a curling iron, such as a Schick Crazy Curl, take a wrapped strand and make the first wave about one and a half inches from the scalp. Continue down the strand, making

waves about one and a half inches apart. Do all strands. Wait ten minutes before removing foil. Then brush hair lightly. (The aluminum foil technique also works well for making standard rolled curls with the curling iron.)

Mitt Curls

Here is a hair-drying technique, rather than a setting technique, that allows you to obtain maximum curl and volume from your hair. All you need, explains Luis Llongueras, who uses it on his own curly hair, is a washcloth mitt. Towel-dry your hair to the point where it is just damp. Then put on the washcloth mitt and, with the palm of your hand, dry your hair with ten circular motions clockwise, followed by ten circular motions counterclockwise. Do this all over your head until the hair is dry. Then brush lightly.

The Guerlain Salon. *Here I found the Paris beauty salon of my imagination: a grand reception room with crystal chandeliers, Oriental rugs, Louis XV-style furnishings, and an atmosphere of tranquility and refinement. Photograph by G. Rouget.*

The Gold-Toned Face. *Harmonized make-up from Thibault at Carita. To achieve this warm, sunny daytime look, you need:* foundation base—*golden beige;* blusher—*apricot or peach;* lipstick—*brick;* lip pencil—*chestnut brown or brick;* eye shadows—*golden brown for lids, medium brown for brow bone. Illustration by Thibault.*

The Rose-Toned Face. *An evening look, with colors cool as moonlight. For this harmonized makeup, also by Thibault, you need:* foundation base—*rosy beige;* blusher—*bordeaux or dusty rose;* lipstick and lip pencil—*wine or plum;* eye shadows—*smoky grey mixed with a little violet for lids, and a touch of rosy beige under the eyebrow. Illustration by Thibault.*

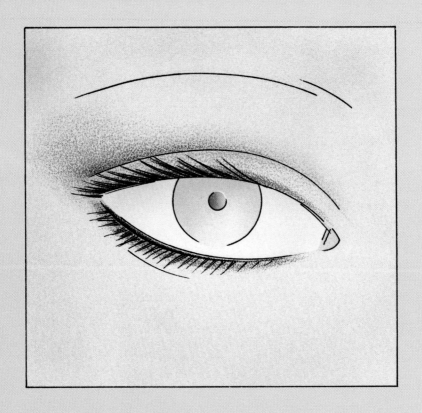

The Eye, à la Française. *The French woman makes up her eyes with great care, accentuating them to their best advantage.* Eye shadow *extends beyond the eye, almost to the end of the eyebrow.* Upper and lower lids *are lined with black, brown or blue pencil, or combination. The* inside lower lid *is lined with black, grey, or blue pencil.* Eyelashes *are coated with at least two applications of black, brown or midnight-blue mascara.*

Recipe for a Basic Makeup. *A simple plan from Olivier Echaudemaison, for which you need foundation base, translucent powder, two eye shadows (one a dark neutral, the other pink or beige), mascara and lipstick. As you apply shadows, look at yourself in profile in a mirror. The line of the eye shadow must always go up, never down.*

Makeup for Electric Light. *Incandescent light tends to wash out color, says Jean-Pierre Fleurimon. Under electric light use bright, clear pinks or reds for lipstick and blusher, true browns or blues for eye shadow.*

Makeup for Fluorescent Light. *To counteract the effects of this cold light, which shows up imperfections and fatigue, choose warm colors—coral, mandarin red, tomato for lipstick and blusher, gold-frosted shadows for your eyes. Lips should be carefully outlined.*

Makeup for Candlelight. *This most flattering light touches everyone with a romantic glow. To contrast with the golden cast of the light, use soft, muted blue-toned colors, such as rose, plum, mauve, cherry or lavender. Use a little more blusher than usual to accentuate the contours of your face.*

Vertical Drying

Luis Llongueras offers another hair-drying tip, this for longer, curly or wavy hair. Instead of blow-drying your hair with the dryer at the top or side of your head (which blows the hair up or back), tilt your head to the side, with the hair hanging down free, and blow-dry with the dryer positioned under the ends of the hair. To dry the back of your hair, tip your head forward and bring your hair over the top of your head, in front of your face. This is most comfortable to do if you are sitting in a chair. Again, dry this portion of your hair with the dryer aimed up from the ends of your hair. With this technique, the hair dries in its most natural position, curling and waving in its own pattern.

Classic Styles to Do or Have Done

Hairstyles and trends evolve and change with every season, as does fashion. But as with fashion, there are classic styles which, surviving the whims of designers and the fashion press, always seem to look just right, year in and year out. What follows are a selection of perennially "in" hairdos, and how to achieve them.

Timeless Cuts

There are very few cuts that do not look dated within five or ten years. But there are two that have withstood the test of time. One, the Chanel cut, a long-standing favorite at Alexandre's, has been fashionable for fifty years. The other, popular for over twenty years, is sometimes referred to as the Jean Seberg cut (remember Joan of Arc?)—super-short and fitting the head like a cap. You will never be *démodé* with either of these cuts.

97

The Chanel Cut is flattering for oval, heart-shaped and long faces. It does not work well with round or square faces. Bangs are combed forward from the center of the head and cut just above the eyebrows, extending all the way back to the temples. The base is blunt-cut straight across, with the back a quarter to a half inch shorter than the sides, and turned slightly under. The Chanel cut is attractive combed straight down on all sides, or with the hair just in front of the ears pulled back with a comb or barrette.

The Jean Seberg Cut is best for a woman with a small head and even features. It gives an almost angelic, fragile, saintly look to the women who wear it. In Paris I saw it on women from eighteen years old to their late forties. The Jean Seberg is usually parted low on the side, with each strand of hair cut exactly the same length as every other.

Your hairstyle should be carefully chosen to frame your face.

Three Carita Chignons

There is nothing as feminine and ladylike as a beautifully wrapped chignon. And you don't always need long hair to create one. With medium-length hair and a small hairpiece you can produce a variety of elegant looks with very little effort. (You can buy a good, synthetic hairpiece for the price of having your hair done. Try out several small, neat styles at a department store or your hairdresser's.)

Chignon Madame Giscard D'Estaing This simple, graceful chignon was designed by Christophe Carita for the First Lady of France. It's not difficult to achieve yourself, but it does require that you buy a small, braided hairpiece, ten to twelve inches long and about two inches wide.

1. Part your hair behind your ears, dividing the hair into two sections. The part should extend from one ear to the other in approximately the line of the braid.

2. Comb the front section smoothly back, teasing a little if necessary for control, and fix the hair at the part with bobby pins. (If your hair is long, turn it under at the part, and fix with bobby pins.)

3. Attach the braid to your hair with bobby pins and hairpins, following the line of the part. The braid should be attached on its side, rather than flat down, so that it sits on the back of your head like a little crown. This gives the chignon greater volume and makes the pattern of the braid more visible.

4. Now comb up the second section of your hair, again teasing if necessary. Bring the hair over the base of the braid and attach the ends neatly under the top of the braid.

5. Spray hair lightly so that no little wisps can escape.

Couture French Twist; This is a contemporary, asymmetrical version of the classic French twist, and is particularly attractive on a woman with a

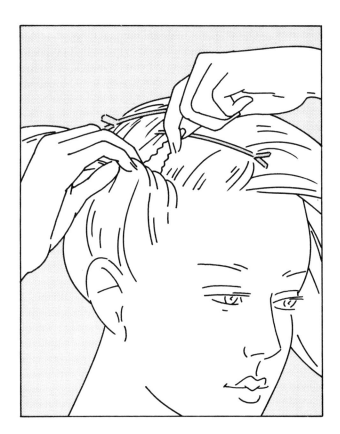

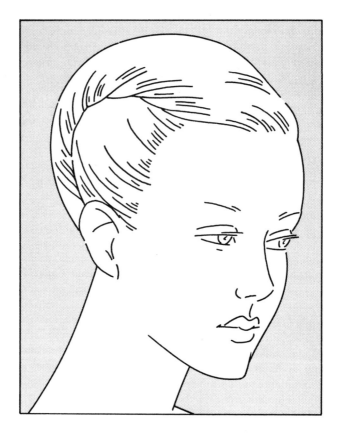

long neck. It works best with chin- to shoulder-length hair.

1. Part your hair on one side of your head, from the forehead all the way back to the neck.

2. Draw up all hair on the side of the part closest to the ear, twist it under, press flat and pin it with bobby pins and hairpins. While you are doing this, keep the hair on the other side of the part out of the way with clips.

3. Now take the hair on the other side of the part and tease it slightly. Then smooth it over the part and turn it under into the twist, directly over the pins holding the first section of hair. Fix the twist with hairpins. Spray lightly to hold.

Round Chignon. Madame Giscard D'Estaing often wears her hair in this neat, understated chignon during the day.

1. Draw all your hair back and divide into three sections, as though you were going to braid it. It helps to tease and spray each section lightly for control. Hold the sections apart with large clips.

2. Take the middle section and turn the ends up and under, fixing them with bobby pins to make a small bun.

3. Bring the right section over the middle, under and around, and fix on the right side, tucking in the ends under the top of the middle section.

4. Bring the left section over the middle, around and under, and fix on the left side, tucking the ends in and under itself, near the top of the middle section.

5. Spray lightly to hold.

Louis G.'s Instant Chignons

Louis G. often uses small hairpieces to dress up the short, casual cuts he does for everyday. Here are two of his favorite styles.

Basic Chignon: This is the simplest chignon you can make. You will need a small, round hairpiece, either twisted, braided or a combination—wrapped center, braided outside.

1. Draw all your hair smoothly back, and attach with bobby pins. If there are any loose wisps, spray them and comb them back carefully.

2. Attach the hairpiece at the back of the head, making sure that all pins are covered. You can accessorize your hairpiece according to the occasion: wind a silver or gold thread through the strands, braid in a

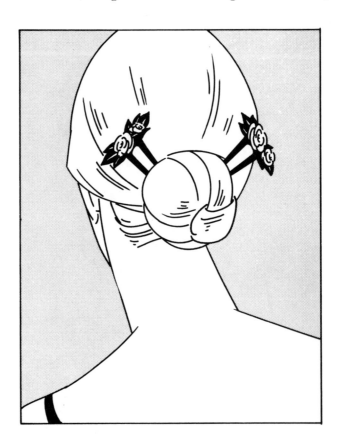

ribbon to match your dress, or decorate with a graceful antique comb, a funny pin, a small feather or anything that suits your fancy.

Torsade: The exquisite style shown below is done with a twisted, two-strand hairpiece on a model with chin-length hair. If you can't find a pre-twisted hairpiece like this (called a *torsade*), buy a hairpiece that is long, loose and unstyled. Then divide it into two strands and twist each strand around your finger like a rope. Then twist the two twisted strands tightly around each other and fasten at the bottom.

1. Comb all hair back from the front of the head, leaving a strand loose in front of each ear, and pin back with bobby pins. Attach the twisted *torsade* to the back of the head, making sure that all the bobby pins are covered. Fix torsade with bobby pins and hairpins.

2. Tease and spray the two remaining strands at the front of the head lightly. Comb them back and over the ends of the *torsade* and tuck them inside the hairpiece, fixing them with hairpins.

The look for evening is elegant and raffine.

Contemporary Updos from Patrick Alès

There are many new ways of twisting, wrapping and attaching your hair for a young, fresh look. These three, from Patrick Alès, were created by in-house star, Romain.

Front Chignon

This is the classic chignon in reverse.

1. Lean forward and brush all your hair from the back of your head to the front.

2. Gather the hair in the center of the forehead, or slightly to the side, over one eyebrow. Twist the hair like a rope, then wrap it around itself, tucking the ends under and attaching the chignon with bobby pins and hairpins. This style is sometimes done leaving little wisps of hair free around the hairline, from one ear to the other, or all around the head.

Banded Ponytail

Here's another striking summer style. A banded ponytail is also a clever way of keeping your hair looking neat and presentable when you're giving it a midsummer oil conditioning treatment, or after you've come out of the pool.

1. Divide your hair, wet or dry, into four equal sections from the front of your head to the back, by making three parts across your head from one side to the other. Clip each section to keep it separate.

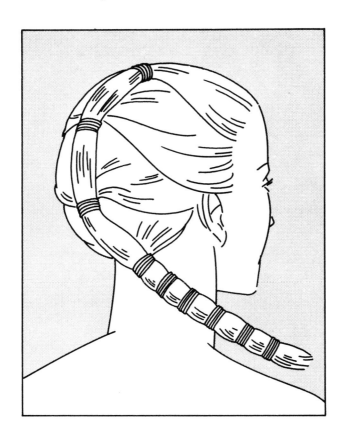

2. Gather the hair of the first section at the front of your head and, with a brightly colored, covered elastic, make a ponytail.

3. Gather the hair of the second section, incorporating the ponytail of the first section, and make another ponytail.

4. Gather the hair of the third section and, with the ponytail of the second section, make another ponytail.

5. Repeat with the last section of hair.

6. Wrap the last ponytail, at even intervals of about three quarters of an inch, with colored elastics or thread.

Wrapped Corn Rows

This style is African-inspired and exotic. It's perfect for medium-length hair, and although it is time-consuming to do, it can last for several days. Try it for a run of summer festivities.

1. Divide hair into five equal sections with parts from the forehead to the neck.

2. At this point you will need a yarn needle threaded with a long, thick strand of colorful or metallic thread. Start twisting the hair of one section from front to back. After you have done about an inch, take the needle and thread, knotted at the end, and stitch the thread around the twist. Then continue to twist the hair another inch, and stitch. Twist and stitch until you reach the nape of your neck. Wrap the thread around several times, knot it neatly, hide the end and finish off.

3. Repeat above for the other four sections.

4. You can use your imagination for how you finish off the five wrapped rows. You can braid each of the ends, weaving in a strand of thread; or wrap them tightly in metallic thread; or leave them loose; or loop them under and attach with bobby pins.

V
Your Body

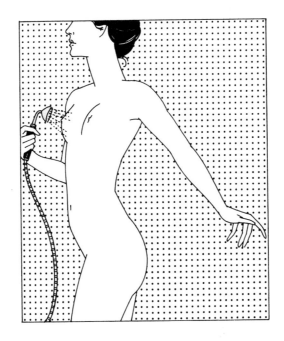

The Paris beauty *instituts* are extremely imaginative and original when it comes to thinking up *soins du corps*—treatments for the body. You can have your whole body coated with a mask of deep-green sea mud from the waters off of Perpignan; be massaged by a powerful current of pulsating air; have a total body peel with vegetable enzymes; or let your muscles be exercised electrically while you lie still. (Electrical apparatus is widely used, and some methods actually approach what we would consider physical therapy. Passive body treatments are still more popular than active exercise.) You can also have your varicose veins treated in a pair of giant, inflatable booties, your breasts massaged with a "toning" oil or your hands conditioned with a paraffin mask.

My own experiences in the realm of body treatments were the most fascinating part of my sojourn in Paris. For while I was familiar with facials, professional makeup sessions and, of course, haircuts, before I came to Paris, body treatments such as breast toning, cellulite reduction and antivaricose vein programs were completely foreign to me, part of an incredible new world. It is here that French beauty care differs most radically from ours. Body treatments other than massage have yet to make a dent in the American beauty business. But in Paris alone, 450

115

institut de beauté owners make a substantial living improving imperfect bodies (and helping a few perfect ones stay that way).

I can't vouch for the long-term effectiveness of the treatments that I had because, at the most, I was only able to fit each of them into my schedule two or three times. In most cases it would be necessary to undergo a series of eight or ten treatments to see a real difference. But I can tell you that the short-term benefits are wonderful. After almost every treatment, I felt better than when I went in, which, as the French say is *déjà pas mal*—already not bad.

The breast-care treatment at Clarins, to firm and tone the breasts, was a revelation to me: You could actually pay the equivalent of twelve dollars and have someone massage your breasts with herbal-scented oil for thirty minutes, pure and simple, no strings attached, and all in the name of beauty. What a joy! It hardly matters whether it's effective or not. The treatment takes place in a neat orange and white cabin, with the client reclining in a terry-cloth-covered *fauteuil*—the oversize, reclining armchair popular in many salons. The oil used (during my treatment by specialist Dominique) is described in Clarins literature as being specially formulated to penetrate the skin, firming, toning and reinforcing the elasticity of the tissues. Ingredients include rosemary, sage, mint and vitamin E. The massage is gentle, using a variety of techniques from broad, smooth strokes to light tapping and tiny pinches. (And, yes, erotic sensations are difficult to ignore.) After the massage the skin of your breasts is pink, smooth and satiny. At the end of my half hour, Dominique asked with a smile, "Not too disagreeable?"

In the city of Paris, where women are more obsessed with the size of their hips than anywhere else on earth, I experienced three different anticellulite treatments. The first one I tried, during a visit to the Ingrid Millet Institut, is called *ionisation,* or electrotherapy. The treatments are given on the lower level, in one of the unusual, stone-walled rooms with vaulted ceilings which resemble the cells of medieval monks. In the *ionisation* process your thighs, hips or whatever area is afflicted with the lumpy, "orange-peel" fat called cellulite are covered with a cream designed to be absorbed by the skin and break up stored fat. Then the areas are wrapped in fabric-covered rectangles that look like heating pads. These rectangles are electrically charged with a very low current.

116

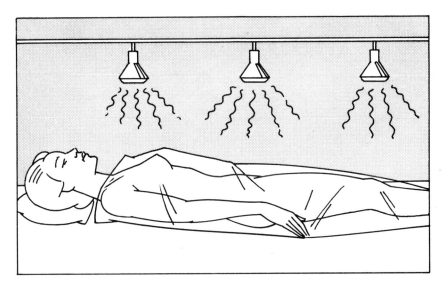

The electricity, it was explained to me, helps the cream to penetrate and also causes the fat to disperse. Electrotherapy is not really uncomfortable, but your skin does feel warm and prickly while the *ionisation* is going on.

My second cellulite treatment took place at the Institut Béatrice Braun. This technique involves infrared lights. For the first ten minutes of the treatments you lie under four infrared lamps, in order to warm the skin, open the pores, and prepare it for the fat-fighting fluid called Silico Mincil that comes next. After the fluid is applied, you are wrapped in a clear plastic sheet, and you bake away under the lights for another twenty minutes. This treatment I found very relaxing. It also left my skin feeling soft and silky.

Drainothérapie, the last cellulite treatment I underwent, is a rhythmic air massage developed and performed at Clarins. Clarins claims that one *drainothérapie* session is as effective as sixty manual massages. They could be right. For this treatment you must hold a plastic shield in front of your face and wear earplugs, so powerful and noisy is the vacuum cleanerlike apparatus.

For forty minutes your cellulite is pummeled with a mighty current of air, strong enough to lift your leg up by itself. Your skin literally ripples and waves under its force. *Drainothérapie* is not pleasant like a massage. Rather, it is in the realm of discomfort, but not quite at the threshold of

When it comes to treatments for the body, the instituts *are imaginative and original.*

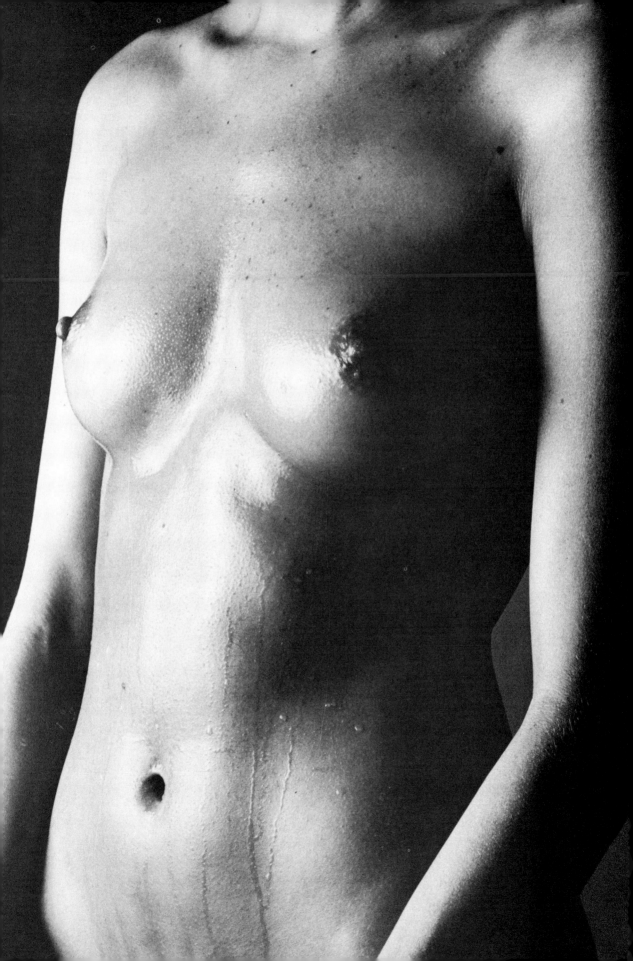

pain. But I would guess that, with two *drainothérapie* sessions a week over two months—the recommended schedule—cellulite doesn't stand a chance.

The leg treatments at the Institut des Jambes are very specialized. They were not developed to beautify legs per se, but to relieve circulation-based problems such as varicose veins and edema. If the legs become more attractive in the process, *tant mieux*—so much the better. The two major treatments at the Institut are the Frigibas and the Legpump. I was curious to try both. In a typical treatment session, given in the pleasant blue and white cabins, you would have twenty minutes of the Legpump, followed by twenty minutes of the Frigibas.

The Legpump consists of a huge pair of seven-league inflatable booties, attached to an automated air pump. The booties, when slipped on, cover your legs up to the thighs. During the session you lie on a padded treatment table. The therapist switches on the pump, and compressed air pulses into the booties, surrounding the troubled appendages with a light, undulating air pressure. The air, which imperceptibly increases in pressure over the twenty minutes, gently massages the legs without harming fragile veins and capillaries. The circulation is stimulated when sluggish blood and retained water are

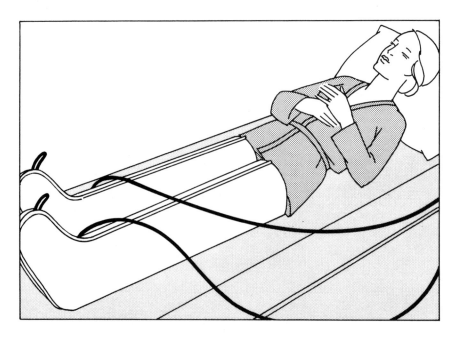

pumped from the legs toward the torso. I found the sensation of the Legpump very odd. At first it felt as though my legs were floating up and away from me. Then, during the last ten minutes, it seemed as though the upper half of my body were getting bigger, the lower half smaller, like a balloon being squeezed from one end. Did anyone ever explode? I lay there and mused on the possibility.

The Frigibas are heavy, opaque black stockings which are impregnated with a special hypothermatic liquid developed to lower the temperature of problem legs (usually four to ten degrees above normal) back to 98.6. After the Legpump, my attendant Myriam soaked a pair of the Frigibas with the liquid and slipped them on. Ugh. Cold, wet stockings on warm, dry legs. A hot-water bottle was then placed on my stomach (to keep the body warm), my legs were wrapped in vinyl and I was covered with a blue and white plaid blanket. After about five minutes I began to experience a bizarre, simultaneous hot/cold sensation in my legs that continued almost until the end of the treatment. Then, during the last three or four minutes, the cold finally vanquished the hot and I began to shiver. When the vinyl was removed, my legs and feet felt very cold, but, strangely, when I touched them with my hand they were warm. This sensation lasted almost an hour, with my legs feeling cold, but warm to the touch. I know these treatments sound a little strange, but they are among the most legitimate in the city; all procedures done at the Institut des Jambes have been carefully tested in hospitals, and the Frigibas have received the approval, or *visa,* required for chemical treatments from the French ministry of health.

Like the Institut des Jambes, many Paris *instituts de beauté* work in conjunction with doctors and hospitals to develop their methods. When it comes to body treatments, the French want to be medically correct.

How to Care for Your Breasts

It's a popular belief, at least in this country, that there's not much you can do to improve your breasts. Clarins disagrees. According to Madame Eliane Pietralonga, a registered nurse who's the *directrice* of the Paris salon, you can have terrible, droopy breasts at twenty or marvelous breasts at fifty or sixty, depending on the kind of care you give them.

To care for your breasts properly, says Madame Pietralonga, you must first understand their characteristics and construction. The breasts, she explains, are not attached to the chest, but rather are suspended from above and held in place by a "natural bra" of muscles which fan out from the neck to the chest. The breast itself consists of a mammary gland couched in adipose (fatty) tissue, which gives the breast its volume, and is surrounded by an envelope of skin, which gives the breast its form. Effective breast care comes down to two major considerations: (1) maintaining the elasticity and tone of the "natural bra" and (2) keeping the adipose tissue as firm as possible. Here is counsel from Clarins on the care and preservation of your breasts.

The bra that you wear is extremely important to the maintenance of your breasts. After all, your breasts are contained and immobilized in this garment twelve to sixteen hours a day, 365 days a year, from the age of thirteen or fourteen on. Your bra must be perfectly fitted, very supple and stretchy, even for heavy breasts, so that the whole breast is encompassed and supported. The breasts should be gently held up, but not pulled up, stresses Madame Pietralonga. The bra should not be low-cut (presses into delicate breast tissue) or too tight, and it should not leave marks on your shoulders.

Clarins advises a cold-water shower for your breasts after your normal bath or shower. This might be hard to get used to, but Clarins is very convincing about the beneficial effects of cold water on the adipose tissue, tightening and toning it. So, aim the shower head at your upper torso, or with a hand-held shower head, zero in on your breasts, turn on the cold water for one minute and grit your teeth. Or, after you come

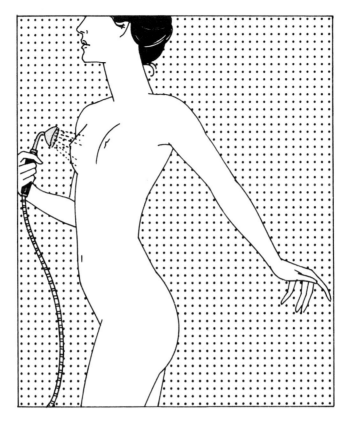

out of the tub, apply cold water from the tap to your breasts three or four times with a washcloth.

Avoid hot baths. They distend the tissues and cause breasts to sag. Instead, take tepid, body-temperature baths, and stay in the tub only ten minutes.

During your bath or shower, use a natural-textured "friction mitt" all over to stimulate your skin and circulation.

Before retiring, or after your bath, apply a rich moisturizer to your breasts, in circular, inside-to-outside motions. Then do this litte treatment: For one minute, give your breasts tiny, almost delicate pinches (i.e., with your thumb and forefinger take a very small amount of flesh and pinch very lightly, pulling upward at the same time, until the skin slips out of your grasp). Repeat this all over your breast. This is done in the breast treatments at the salon, and helps to stimulate circulation in the breasts, which helps to tone them up.

Bad posture also makes the breasts sag. If your back is rounded, if your chest is hollow, if you tend to hunch, make a concerted effort to straighten up—head up, back straight, shoulders back. You will notice an instant breast lift.

Swimming, particularly the appropriately named breaststroke, is the ideal exercise for maintaining beautiful breasts. It combines the toning effect of cold water with constant rhythmic movements that strengthen the "natural bra." Gymnastics—hanging from bars, swinging from rings, handstands, cartwheels—are also effective, although much more physically demanding.

There are two simple exercises you can do at home to help firm up your body's "natural bra":

1. Looking in the mirror, contract all the muscles of your neck and jaw until you see your breasts rise slightly with the movement. Then relax. Repeat this exercise for one minute, every morning and evening.

2. Bring your hands in front of your chest in a prayer position, elbows straight out to the side. Press your palms together as hard as you can for five seconds, then relax. Repeat twenty times, morning and evening. You can feel this working immediately.

Rapid or frequent changes in weight are bad for your whole body, but they are particularly bad for your breasts. If possible, keep your weight stable and avoid crash diets. Pregnancies too close together also take their toll on breasts.

Diets lacking in protein can cause the slackening of breast tissue. So be sure you eat a healthy ration of fish, meat, chicken, eggs and cheese.

If you diet, you must take particular care of your breasts during this period, since there is a tendency for the breasts to become flaccid. So be sure to eat protein, give your breasts cold-water showers, do the pinch treatment and exercise while you are dieting and in the post-diet period, to keep breasts as firm as possible.

Firming Your Upper Arms

One of the most difficult areas of your body to keep firm and slim is the upper arm. But flabby arms, particularly in a bare party dress, can make you look older and slightly frumpy, even if everything else is perfect. Here are two simple exercises to tone the upper arms, practiced by several body-conscious Parisiennes I met. The exercises will also help strengthen the chest's pectoral muscles.

1. For this exercise you will have to buy two small two- to three-pound weights, available at sporting goods stores. Lie on your back on a bench or table and make twenty circular motions backward with straight arms, as though you were doing the backstroke. Repeat in forward direction. Add five rotations a day until you are doing fifty. Continue this exercise every day to prevent arms from reverting to flab once they are toned. (You can do this same exercise without weights, but it's much less effective.)

2. Or try this: Walk around a (carpeted) room on your hands and knees, keeping your palms turned out to the side for the first half of the walk, then turn inward for the last half. Do this exercise five minutes a day, preferably in conjunction with the above exercise.

Caring for Problem Legs

The Institut des Jambes operates on one basic premise, verified by the doctors who founded the center, and that is: the temperature of problem legs—those with varicose veins, cellulite, edema or broken capillaries—is from two to ten degrees higher than the normal 98.6, depending on the severity of the problem. The temperature is higher because the veins are distended, circulation is poor and there is too much blood in the area. The thrust of the two major treatments at the Institut des Jambes—the Frigibas and the Legpump—is to lower the leg temperature and improve the circulation.

Madame Delille, the *directrice* of the Institut, says that almost 90 percent of all women have some enlarged veins. This, she explains, is a result of pregnancy and also because women are so often on their feet, during the day at jobs that require them to stand or working in the home, and at night preparing dinner and caring for children.

Treating serious leg problems is not really a do-it-yourself operation. But if you have broken capillaries or varicose veins, there are things you should know and a few things you can do, suggested by Madame Delille, to avoid making the problems worse and perhaps alleviating them to some degree.

Don'ts

1. Don't take hot baths. They make the body warmer and enlarge already dilated veins.

2. Avoid alcohol if possible. Alcohol also raises body temperature.

3. Cut way down on tea, coffee, pepper and tobacco, all stimulants that make you warmer.

4. Cut down on salt, since it causes water retention and tends to swell limbs.

5. Avoid all constraining articles of clothing, such as girdles, tight pants, tight pantyhose—anything that inhibits circulation.

6. Avoid crossing your legs. This also inhibits circulation.

7. Avoid lying directly in the sun. Even though a tan covers unattractive varicosities, the sun dilates the veins and may make the problem worse.

8. Avoid massages on your legs. A massage traumatizes already fragile vessels, and can cause them to break.

Do's

1. Take lukewarm, body-temperature baths. The idea may not appeal to you, but you will discover that they are very relaxing.

2. Walk as much as possible.

3. Do light exercise that doesn't put too much strain on your legs, such as swimming or yoga.

4. Morning and evening, and in between whenever possible, do ten minutes of the following exercises: Lying on your back, legs and hips in the air with your hands supporting the small of your back, do twenty bicycle movements, followed by ten back-and-forth scissor kicks and then ten side-to-side scissor kicks. Repeat series for ten minutes. These exercises are good for the circulation, and make the blood descend from the legs to the torso.

An Anticellulite Program

Cellulite, the puckery fat that develops around hips, thighs and stomach, is a problem that affects a majority of women over the age of fourteen. It's a fat that is mixed with body wastes, and it is harder and more compressed than fat on other parts of your body. Cellulite fat accumulates and then presses through the skin's connective tissue like putty pressing through a screen, giving the skin a "quilted" look. Cellulite is caused by a variety of factors, including hormonal problems, constipation, heredity, poor diet, lack of exercise, even too much exercise (if it puts excessive pounding stress on your legs). Constricting clothing, such as girdles, tight pants, tight pantyhose and tight boots can also contribute to the formation of cellulite by inhibiting circulation. This annoying fat often starts with the onset of puberty and develops slowly and insidiously. Once it appears, it's almost impossible to get rid of completely. But it can be controlled, reduced and in some cases prevented with a combination of diet, exercise and care that can be done at home.

At the Institut Béatrice Braun, Béatrice and her husband, Dr. Marcel Braun, have done extensive research into the causes and cures for cellulite. At the Institut you would be treated by *ionisation* or infrared lights, combined with either Silico Mincil or Lipolysium, two exclusive Braun products. (Dr. Braun does not believe that massage, either in the salon or at home, is very effective for diminishing cellulite. "The only one who loses pounds and inches in the process," he says, "is the masseur.")

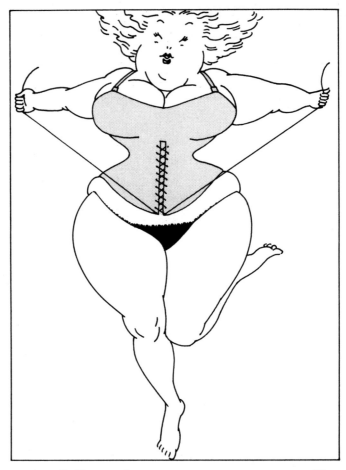

To conquer cellulite at home, you must put yourself on a strict routine. I asked the Brauns to outline a simple, at-home program to reduce and control cellulite. The program they gave me breaks down into three areas: diet, dressing and exercise.

Diet

1. A proper diet to avoid or reduce cellulitic buildup must be based on lean proteins—broiled meats other than pork or lamb, fish, eggs, chicken and cottage cheese.

2. Avoid salt and salty foods, which cause the body to retain water—preserved meats such as bacon or ham, tuna canned in oil, peanuts, potato chips, packaged sauces, pickles.

3. Cut down on carbohydrates—bread, rice, pasta, cereals.

4. Cut out sugar and sweets—candy, honey, cakes, ice cream, jam, fruits in syrups.

5. Never skip a meal. Your body will be much healthier if it is regularly digesting moderate-size meals rather than one or two large ones. When your digestive system is working smoothly, body wastes will not accumulate.

6. Eliminate or drastically reduce alcoholic beverages, which are high in sugar content and also put a strain on the body's filtration and elimination system. For a before-meal drink, try Perrier water or club soda with a slice of lemon or lime.

7. Drink a minimum of one to two quarts of water a day. According to Dr. Braun, this is the most important of his alimentary recommendations. Water aids digestion and keeps your system clean.

So remember: *no* to alcohol, sugar, salt and fatty foods; *yes* to lots of water and lean protein.

Dressing

1. Don't try to squeeze yourself into skinny-legged pants if you do not have skinny legs.

2. Don't wear a girdle.

3. Make sure that your pantyhose are ample and do not constrict your waist and hips.

4. Avoid knee-high stockings. They tend to cut off circulation at the knee.

5. Avoid boots that bind your legs.

6. Do not sit with your legs crossed, a position that inhibits circulation in your legs.

Exercises

The best exercises to trim down the hip and thigh area are those which involve gentle stretching movements, based on yoga. (More violent, demanding exercise, such as running, can put too much stress on the legs, and end up making the problem worse. The benefits of mild exercise are twofold, explains Dr. Braun. It stimulates circulation, which

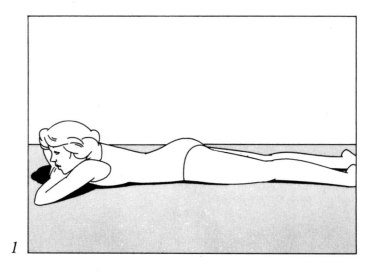

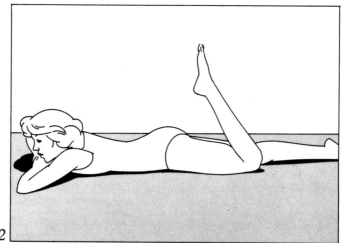

helps decongest the cellulitic area, and it also firms the muscles, which, because they sag, can accentuate "saddlebags" and droopy buttocks. A sedentary life-style is the major cause of this loss of tone. The Brauns recommend four simple exercises, two for the buttocks and two for the thighs, to practice daily.

For the buttocks:
1. Lie on your stomach with your arms bent, elbows out to the side,

3

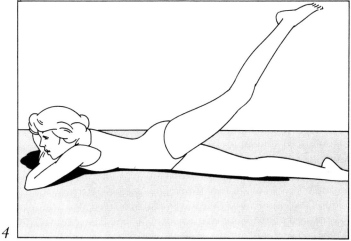

4

hands clasped in front of you and your chin resting on your hands (position 1). Bend one leg at the knee, toe pointing toward the ceiling (position 2). Raise that leg off the floor in the bent position as high as it will go (position 3). Then extend the leg straight out, toe pointed, as high as it will go (position 4), and bounce leg up five times. Now return the leg to position 3, then to position 2, and finally back to the starting position. Repeat with the other leg. Do this exercise, slowly and fluidly, four more times with each leg.

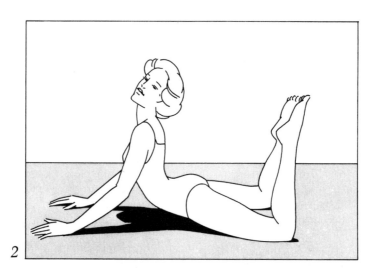

2. Still lying on your stomach, bend your arms in front of you, palms flat on the floor, and spread your legs about a foot apart. Raise your torso off the floor. (Position 1.) Then slowly bend your legs at the knee and bring your toes as close as they will go to the back of your head. (Position 2.) Holding this position, make three circles with your head clockwise, then three counterclockwise. Now return your legs to the starting position and relax your torso. Repeat ten times.

For the thighs

1. Kneel on the floor, your knees about a foot apart, your arms by your sides, about six inches out from your body. Keeping your back straight, lean your whole body back toward your feet as far as you can go. (All the tension in your body should be centered in your thighs.) Now return your body slowly to the starting position. Remember to keep your back straight. Repeat ten times, each time trying to go a little farther back.

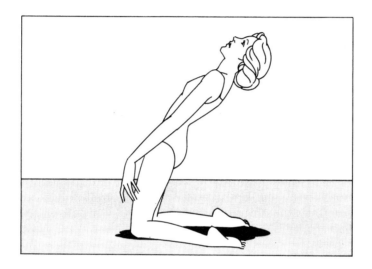

2. Sit on the floor, with your back straight, legs extended out in front of you, your arms extended out to the side at shoulder level (position 1). Bend your knees to your chest until your feet are two inches off the ground (position 2). Then extend your feet straight out in front of you, keeping them at least a foot off the floor (position 3). Hold this position for five seconds. Slowly return to position 2, then the starting position. Repeat ten times.

1

2

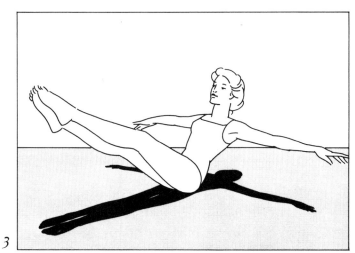

3

135

Going to Extremities: Your Hands and Feet

Your hands and feet are expressive and very visible parts of your body, and should not be ignored in your beauty program. No matter how well dressed you may be, or how beautifully your makeup is applied, you will not look truly *soignée* if your nails are ragged or the polish chipped. Change your polish as often as necessary; it should always look fresh and neat. Schedule a full manicure and a full pedicure at least once a month.

Treatment Mask for Dry, Rough Hands

At the Guerlain salon, very dry hands get a special treatment called a *supermasque*. First your hands are massaged with a very thick, rich cream. Then warm, liquid paraffin wax is brushed on the hands. The paraffin hardens immediately, encasing the hands in hard, airtight wax gloves. This hand *masque* helps the cream penetrate into dry skin very effectively.

After half an hour the wax is removed and the excess cream wiped off, revealing newly softened and smoothed hands. This is not an easy treatment to duplicate at home, but you can get some good results by massaging a rich cream into your hands and then slipping on rubber gloves that have been warmed in hot water, and tying them closed at the wrist. Or use surgical gloves, available at some pharmacies. Leave on for half an hour to an hour, then remove, and wipe off excess cream.

But, you might want to try a real *supermasque*. It's more work and you will need someone to help you briefly, but it's a great deal more effective. Buy a box of pure paraffin (used for canning or candle making) at a hardware store. Melt a bar in the bowl of a double boiler, or in an aluminum pan within a pan filled with water. Remove and let cool to the point where it is very warm and still liquid. (Test the temperature with a drop of wax on your wrist.) Rub a very rich lubricating cream into your hands. Put one hand into the bowl of paraffin and, with a wide pastry brush, smooth the wax over your hand so that the skin down to the wrist is completely covered. Now you will need the help of a friend to do the same thing to the other hand, unless you're very nimble and speedy, and can do both hands yourself before the paraffin hardens. After half an hour (a good time to meditate, since your hands will be completely immobilized), peel off the mask and wipe off the excess cream.

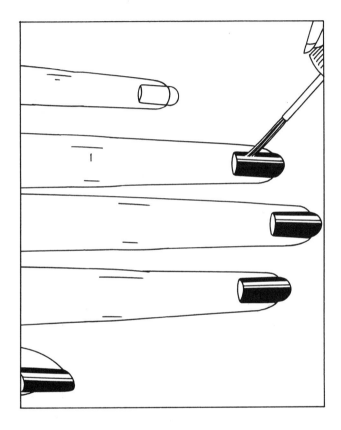

A Manicure Extraordinaire

A manicure at the beautiful Guerlain salon is a luxurious experience. You sit in an upholstered Louis XV-style armchair, surrounded by mahogany-panel walls and graceful floor-to-ceiling windows that open out onto the Champs-Élysées. During the full hour that the manicure takes, you are treated with a calm graciousness, as if you were a familiar, but honored, guest in the house. The manicurists, garbed in neat, pale-blue uniforms, are deferential and soft-spoken. The price for all this elegance I found quite reasonable—about six dollars at the time I was there. You may not be able to have a manicure at Guerlain, but you can do your own, *à la* Guerlain, following the directions of experienced manicurist Pascale:

What you need:

- Nail polish remover
- An emery board
- A bowl of soapy water (use a gentle liquid soap or shampoo)
- Cuticle scissors
- An orangewood stick
- Cotton balls
- Night cream or baby cream
- Hand lotion
- A nail brush
- A pumice stone
- A small hand towel
- Base coat
- Nail polish

What you do:

1. Remove old nail polish, if any.
2. File your nails down to the same length and shape. Pascale says that you should *never* cut your nails, except if they are very long and you want to make them very short. Otherwise, file your nails with an emery board

to complement the shape of your fingers: If you have squarish, flat fingers, the nails should be kept very even and rounded; if your fingers are long and narrow, the nails should be filed in a long elipse. Nails should never come to a point.

3. Soak both hands in lukewarm soapy water for five minutes. At Guerlain they use their own liquid soap, but you can get almost the same effect with baby shampoo—two or three capfuls in a basin or large bowl. After soaking, remove hands and pat dry.

4. Wrap a small, thin wisp of cotton over the dampened end of an orangewood stick, and gently go over each nail to remove dead skin from the sides and bottom. Press as lightly as you can on the nail, particularly near the cuticle. (If you push too hard, you can damage the shape of the nail).

5. With a cuticle scissors, cut the dead skin away from the sides of each nail. Never, cautions Pascale, cut the cuticles. It might look good after the manicure, she explains, but two days later the cuticles will be ragged and dry.

6. At this point, at the salon, you would have mink oil applied to each nail. If you don't happen to have any mink oil handy, use a rich night cream or even baby cream. Rub the cream well into and around each nail with a light back-and-forth massage.

7. Rub your favorite hand cream into your hands until it is absorbed.

8. With a very soft nail brush (the one used at Guerlain has pure silk bristles), brush over each nail.

9. Take a small pumice stone and gently rub it around each nail to remove any last trace of dead skin.

10. Clean under each nail with an orange stick with cotton wrapped over the end.

11. Refile each nail one more time to make sure it is perfectly smooth.

12. With nail polish remover on a piece of cotton, go over each nail to remove all oil or cream. (Polish will not adhere well to the nail if there is any oil on it.)

13. Apply the base coat, let dry for five minutes, then apply the first coat of polish. Wait five minutes, then apply the second coat of polish. When applying polish, never touch the cuticle with the applicator brush. Polish should begin at the very base of the nail, but should not cover any skin.

14. Now have your dinner brought to you on a tray, with a single rose in a silver vase.

Caring for Your Feet

"In general," says pedicure specialist Sylvia, at the Claude Maxime salon, "women tend to neglect their feet. And that's too bad—feet put the finishing touch on personal beauty. If a woman goes out all dressed up, but she has unattractive feet in sandals, one notices and it detracts. When you have pretty, cared-for feet, the rest of you will feel more beautiful. And sexy!"

Here's how to give yourself an effective pedicure, followed by a foot massage, recommended once every three or four weeks. If you have all the equipment listed for the manicure, you have more than everything you need for the pedicure.

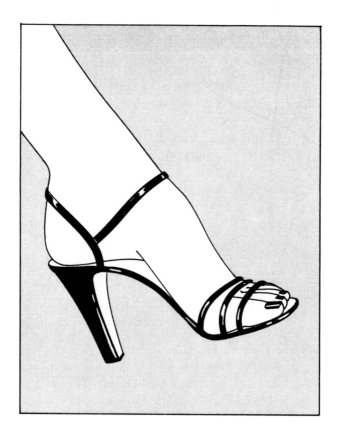

What you do:

1. In a bathtub or basin, soak both your feet in warm water for ten minutes.

2. Remove one foot from the water and pat dry with a towel, leaving the other foot in to soak.

3. With a nail scissors, cut the toenails straight across, not too close to the quick, and not in the corners.

4. With an orangewood stick, clean under each nail and along the sides, pushing away dead skin from the nail. With a cuticle cutter, clip away the dead skin, being careful not to touch the live skin around the nail.

5. With a small pumice stone, rub away the dead skin at heels, calluses and corns.

6. With the orangewood stick, gently push down the skin at the cuticles. Do not press on the quick of the nail. With a cuticle clipper, cut off just the barest excess of dead skin at the cuticle. You must be very careful not to harm the skin that protects the nail.

7. Now put a drop or two of oil (baby oil or coconut oil) on each nail and massage in well to lubricate the nails. Leave on five minutes to absorb, then wipe up excess with cotton balls.

8. Repeat procedure with the other foot.

Foot Massage

1. After the pedicure has been completed, apply a rich body cream or face cream to the top of one foot. With the palms of your hands, massage the cream upward toward your calf, alternating one hand with the other. This motion stimulates circulation and revitalizes tired legs and feet. Do this for three minutes. Repeat with the other foot.

2. Take each toe individually and massage it between your thumb and forefinger. Move the toe from side to side, up and down, then pull it gently straight out.

141

3. With the palm of one hand, massage the sole of each foot, using a firm, fluid motion from the base of the toes to the heel. The stroke should go only in this direction. Massage each foot for one minute.

4. If you want to apply nail polish, remove excess cream or oil from each nail, so that the polish will adhere. Then apply a base coat, followed by two coats of polish.

Daily Foot Care

Marelia, the always-booked pedicurist at the Institut Payot, whose clients come from all over the world, advises a simple daily foot-care routine to keep feet well groomed and callus-free: Every day in your shower or bath, rub your feet all over with a finely textured pumice stone. This way no dead, dry skin can build up and your feet will always be smooth. After you rub your feet dry, apply a moisturizing cream, rubbing it in thoroughly.

Nail Details

French women have more *éclat* than others when it comes to their fingers and toes. For nail polish they prefer bright, clear reds instead of pastel and frosted shades, which are becoming rather *démodé* in Paris. The old forties look of letting the moons show on the fingernails, set off by deep red polish, is making a small comeback among some fashionable Parisiennes, but for the most part the polish is still traditionally applied, two or three coats covering the whole nail.

When you use striking, vibrant colors your nails must be kept in perfect condition, the polish changed often. If you usually use clear or pastel polish, why not take a break from the old standbys and choose a brilliant, pure red for yourself? You'll be surprised how feminine and sexy a little polish can make you feel.

Épilation/Removing Unwanted Hair

In Europe, waxing has long been a more popular way to remove body hair than either shaving or depilatory creams. To many European women, shaving seems unfeminine. And a real bother, too, since it has to be done several times a week to keep stubble-free. French women go to their local salons for a waxing once every month or six weeks, where the *épilation* is usually done with a warm wax. A few women do it at home, with prepared strips of cold wax. The women I know swear that the hair grows back finer and slower the more you wax. And the soft, fine hair that does grow back between waxings doesn't seem to bother them, *or* their men.

I had a very pleasant *épilation* at Guerlain, where they use a pretty, clear-pink wax, which they developed and manufacture. The wax has a special added elastic element which makes it stretchy to the touch as it hardens. This stretchiness makes the hair removal less uncomfortable than with ordinary wax, since the Guerlain wax "gives" a little as it is being pulled off. Each section of your leg or body is waxed twice to make doubly sure that it is smooth and hairless. Guerlain uses five tons of wax a year, heating it up, applying it, stripping it off and throwing it away.

The most unusual *épilation* I encountered was at the Ingrid Millet salon, where Thérèse, a Lebanese-born *esthéticienne*, does a "waxing" with sugar and lemon juice. It's an ancient Lebanese method whereby the sugar is heated with the lemon juice into caramel, then worked into a sticky ball before it hardens. This tacky lump whisks off the hair faster and just as effectively, if not more so, than wax, and it leaves the skin very soft and smooth, not to mention sweet.

With the recipe from Thérèse, I tried five times to duplicate this procedure at home, but it never worked for me. Either it hardened instantly into rock candy, or turned into a sticky paste in my hand. And I did everything I saw Thérèse do—except succeed.

The best way to try an *épilation* at home is with prepared strips of cold wax from the Ella Baché company. Baché products are widely available in U.S. pharmacies. There are small prepared strips for facial waxing and larger, longer strips for leg waxing. You press them on and pull them off almost in one stroke. The discomfort lasts only for a split second. The best part about waxing, of course, is that you don't have to worry about removing the hair again for weeks.

Natural Diuretics

Chemical diuretics, which cause retained water in your body to be released, are very harsh on the system and sometimes have bad side effects, such as liver and kidney damage or dehydration. There are natural products, however, which relieve bloat almost as effectively as their chemical counterparts and are much gentler for your body. Here are two healthy ways to flush excess water from your system, perhaps before the onset of your period, or to kick off a new diet.

Diuretic Béatrice Braun:

Boil two pounds of leeks in two quarts of water for half an hour. Set aside the leeks and put the broth in a pitcher or bottle and let it cool. Drink *only* this during one entire day, and drink it all. In the evening, eat one serving of the boiled leeks as a salad with lemon juice or vinaigrette dressing (a popular French appetizer). Be sure to pick a day when you can relax, because you will be spending much of your time traveling back and forth to the bathroom. Beatrice Braun says that this concoction will rid your body of at least two pounds of water. Many of her clients use this method one day every week, to keep from bloating.

Diuretic Herbier de Provence:

Verveine (verbena) tea and the herbs rosemary, cumin and fennel are all diuretics. Take one teaspoon of any of the above, or perhaps a mixture of the herbs with a sprig of mint, and add to a cup of boiling water. Remove from the heat and let the liquid sit for ten minutes. Filter or strain into a cup, then sip slowly. If you don't like the flavor, you can add a teaspoon of honey. Drink this herbal tea twice a day, morning and evening, for four days.

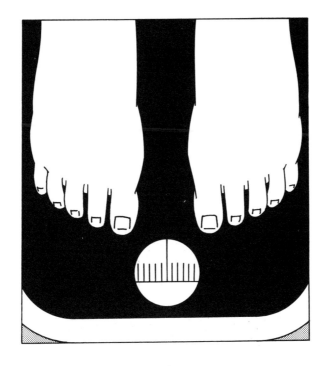

Dieting, Paris Style

The importance of your diet to your total well-being cannot be emphasized too strongly. What you eat plays a major role in the appearance of your skin, the condition of your hair and the way you feel. We all know we should eat in moderation of a well-balanced diet, but many of us stray from the ideal. We overindulge, our weight shoots up and we battle it down again with another diet. Although the Paris *instituts de beauté* do not usually specialize in weight-loss problems, one of their leading exponents, Ingrid Millet, has some sage, Gallic-flavored advice for stabilizing your weight and staying fit. And Maigrir, Rester Mince, a program that *does* specialize in problems of overweight, offers a sound, healthy diet for taking weight off and keeping it off.

A Daily Routine to Keep You Young and Slim

Ingrid Millet is in superb condition. Just entering her seventh decade, she is as trim, chic and attractive as women half her age. When I asked her what her secret was, she replied that it was simply the way she ate and exercised. She graciously agreed to share her personal and very healthy daily regimen with me. Perhaps this is the way you manage to look forty-five when you are past sixty.

1. First thing in the morning, as soon as you get out of bed, drink a large glass of (mineral) water at room temperature. (Ingrid keeps a bottle of mineral water on her night table.)

2. Wash your face and brush your teeth.

3. Do twenty minutes of stretching exercises and bent-knee sit-ups. (Ingrid cautions that most women after forty or fifty should avoid straight-leg sit-ups. They're too hard on the back.) While you exercise, breathe through your nose, and remember to breathe regularly.

4. Shower.

5. Breakfast: Half a grapefruit, a hard-boiled egg, a slice of toast with a dab of butter, a slice of Swiss cheese, and a huge cup of tea.

6. Lunch: A small slice of cold meat, fish or chicken (or, if she's in the United States, cottage cheese), a fresh green vegetable like string beans or a salad, and two large glasses of mineral water.

7. Dinner: A small piece of broiled meat like steak or veal, fresh cooked vegetables or a salad, followed by fresh fruit. (It's best to have one cooked vegetable and one raw vegetable per day in your diet. If you had a salad for lunch, have cooked vegetables for dinner, or vice versa.) You can see that all the meals in Ingrid's diet are balanced and approximately the same size.

8. Walk an hour a day. It's perfect for respiration and circulation.

9. Make love. "It's very important for a woman to make love," says Ingrid, "but you don't need my personal program for that. Making love keeps a woman younger. I'm not sure what effect it has on the man . . ."

Ingrid Millet is innovative in the kitchen as well as in the Institut. Here are two delicious dietetic "fakes" she devised, one a mayonnaise substitute for salad dressing and the other a whipped cream substitute for a fruit topping on special occasions.

Mayonnaise Substitute: Mix together a cup of yogurt, a tablespoon of mild mustard and a teaspoon of fresh lemon juice. This is also good as a dietetic dip for raw vegetables.

Whipped Cream Substitute: Slightly heat the whites of six eggs in an aluminum bowl or a pan. Then whip or whisk them up with two tablespoons of heavy cream and ten drops of artificial sweetener.

The Lose Weight, Stay Thin Diet

Maigrir, Rester Mince ("Lose Weight, Stay Thin") is a small weight-loss clinic in an unprepossessing neighborhood of Paris, a few blocks below Montmartre. Although not glamorous, the clinic has been successful because its program is healthy and quick, and the results last. Most clients lose ten to twenty pounds in three weeks, but what Maigrir, Rester Mince considers more important is that they lose inches or "volume" where necessary. The clinic is supervised by two consulting doctors who give each client a battery of tests—blood, urinalysis, electrocardiogram— and then an analysis of her life-style, to determine the kind of diet best suited for her. A large number of the clients who come to the clinic are married women in their early thirties, with one or two children. "Their bodies have modified since they were married," says co-director Ferdi-nand Goyetche. "Their husbands usually make some remark about the great appearance of another woman, and that almost always triggers the decision to do something about themselves."

The Maigrir, Rester Mince program consists of a strict, balanced diet, plus office visits every other day for consultations, weigh-ins, *ionisation* treatments and moral support. No drugs—amphetamines or chemical diuretics—are used to spur weight loss. With medication, explains M. Goyetche, you can have quick weight loss but the body's system becomes unbalanced. And the weight usually returns quickly once the medication is stopped. A person feels depressed from the drugs, and this depression

147

is compounded by regaining weight. "With our program," M. Goyetche says, "the woman stays in perfect health, without feeling depressed or tired, and the weight will stay off afterward with normal eating."

For a weight-loss cure *chez vous*, Maigrir, Rester Mince recommends that you follow their 1,200-calorie diet, with eight "protein days," for one month. This diet is a modified, less-stringent version of the diet they give their clients under supervision. Supplement the diet with one multi-vitamin capsule daily.

Here is the basic plan:

Breakfast:
- Coffee or tea with skim or powdered milk
- Two French *biscottes* (rusks) or four pieces of melba toast with one tablespoon butter

Lunch:
- Three ounces *crudités* (raw vegetables—enough for a small salad plate), with vinegar and one tablespoon oil*
- Three ounces (two small slices) broiled, roasted or baked lean meat or fish
- Six ounces (about one cup) steamed or boiled green vegetables with one teaspoon of butter
- Slice of hard cheese (one ounce)
- One piece of fruit
- One *biscotte* or two slices of melba toast
* Vinegar, garlic, pepper and spices can be used freely. Use salt sparingly.

Dinner:
- *Crudités* (three ounces), with oil and vinegar
- Broiled (or roasted or baked) lean meat or two eggs (three ounces)
- Six ounces of cooked green vegetables with one teaspoon of butter
- One half cup plain yogurt with artificial sweetener, or cottage cheese
- One piece of fruit
- One *biscotte* or two slices of melba toast

The calorie breakdown for the day goes like this:

Skim or powdered milk for coffee	54
Hard cheese	110
Yogurt or cottage cheese	55
Lean meat, fish or eggs	320
Four *biscottes* or eight melba toasts	160
Vegetables	180
Fruits	100
Butter	144
Oil	90
Total calories for day	1,213

This is the diet that you follow five out of seven days every week. Two days a week, but not two consecutive days, you should eat *only* protein—eggs, meat, chicken, fish or hard cheese, as little as possible, but according to your hunger, and drink eight glasses of water a day in addition to coffee or tea. For example, you would follow the prescribed diet Sunday, Tuesday, Wednesday, Friday and Saturday, and on Monday and Thursday you would eat exclusively protein. At the end of this regime you can expect to lose six to ten pounds of real (not water) weight that will stay off.

The portions of the above diet are divided into three meals. If you prefer, you can break the meals down into five or six smaller ones, saving the cheese and *biscotte* from lunch for an afternoon snack, and the fruit and yogurt from dinner for a late-evening snack. However you divide up the menu, do not deviate from the portions or ingredients at all.

After one month of dieting you can begin eating normally again, but with an eye on the scale. A Maigrir, Rester Mince client is advised to establish a weight danger point, three or four pounds above her post-diet weight, beyond which she must not go. If her weight climbs to the danger point, she diets strictly—all proteins, lots of water—for two days to bring her weight down to where it should be. This is a more natural and healthy way to keep your weight stabilized than waiting until you've gained ten or fifteen pounds and dieting for a month. Maigrir, Rester Mince suggests that you make a weight-loss chart like this, to carefully record your weight over a three-month period, from the day you begin your diet. This way you will have a record of your weight loss, with two follow-up months of scrupulous attention to your weight.

Weight-Loss Chart

Pounds*	Month #1				Month #2				Month #3			
	Week 1	2	3	4	1	2	3	4	1	2	3	4
145												
143												
141												
139												
137												
135												
133												
131												
129												
127												
125												
123												
121												
119												
117												
115												

*When you compose this chart, fill in your own thirty-pound range, starting at the top with a weight ten pounds above your present weight and finishing at the bottom twenty pounds below your present weight.

Here is a list of recommended and forbidden foods to consider when you plan your 1,200-calorie days:

Recommended and Forbidden Foods

	Yes	No
Cheese	Cottage cheese, pot cheese, cheddar, Swiss, Monterey Jack, muenster, yogurt	Camembert, Brie, Gourmandise, chèvre, Boursin, Bonbel, cream cheese
Milk	Skim or powder	Whole milk, cream
Meat	Beef, veal, chicken, liver, lean ham, lamb	All meats in sauces, pork, salami, duck
Fish	Sole, trout, flounder, scrod	Salmon, herring, tuna, sardines, mackerel
Eggs	Soft-boiled, hard-boiled, poached	Fried, scrambled, omelets
Vegetables	Tomatoes, zucchini, leeks, cucumbers, lettuce, radishes, green beans, cabbage, spinach, Brussels sprouts	Potatoes, peas, corn, all dried beans
Fruits	Oranges, grapefruit, apples, pears, grapes, pineapple, strawberries, canteloupe	Bananas, all dried fruits, watermelon, nuts
Beverages	Water, tea, coffee	Wine, beer, fruit juice, soft drinks, hard liquor

Maigrir, Rester Mince has put together a week of suggested 1,200-calorie menus, using many of the recommended foods. The menus are simple variations of the basic plan, with one cooked vegetable, one raw vegetable, a meat, fish or egg portion, a cheese and a fruit at every meal. You may also have one *biscotte* or two pieces of melba toast with each lunch and dinner. Breakfast is constant—coffee or tea with skim milk, two *biscottes* or four pieces of melba toast with butter.

Monday

Lunch	*Dinner*
Chilled radishes	Tomato salad
Roast veal	Chopped steak
Steamed carrots	Green beans
Yogurt	Muenster cheese
Baked apple	Sliced oranges

Tuesday

Lunch	*Dinner*
Shredded red cabbage salad	Endive salad
Grilled steak	Filet of sole
Steamed spinach	Grilled green peppers
Cottage cheese	Swiss cheese
Pear	Small bunch of grapes

Wednesday

Lunch	*Dinner*
Cucumber salad	Salad of grated carrots
Two hard-boiled eggs	Sliced lamb
Leeks vinaigrette	Mixed vegetables
Yogurt	Edam cheese
Apple	Two mandarin oranges

152

Thursday

Lunch
Green mixed salad
Roast beef
Baked zucchini
Cheddar cheese
Half a grapefruit

Dinner
Asparagus vinaigrette
Rock Cornish hen
Braised endives
Cottage cheese
Mixed fruit salad

Friday

Lunch
Leeks vinaigrette
Baked haddock
Steamed carrots
Yogurt
Sliced pineapple

Dinner
Hearts of lettuce salad
Sliced boiled ham
Cauliflower
Muenster cheese
Apple compote, prepared with
artificial sweetener

Saturday

Lunch
Green bean salad
Broiled calf's liver
Broiled tomatoes
Edam cheese
Two small tangerines

Dinner
Tomato and pepper salad
Veal *escalope,*
sautéed with lemon juice
Brussels sprouts
Yogurt
Poached pear

Sunday

Lunch
Cauliflower salad
Roast chicken
Green beans
Cottage cheese
Fruit salad

Dinner
Mushrooms vinaigrette
Tournedos, broiled
Steamed zucchini and onion
Swiss cheese
Half a grapefruit

VI
BATH RITES

The bath in France is a lot more than just washing up; it is a ritual, a refuge, a "cure" and, occasionally, an aphrodisiac. French tubs are generously designed, large, long and deep, often with room enough to lounge full-length. Immersed in one, surrounded by warm water, steam and fragrant bubbles, the little, nagging troubles of the day seem to melt away. The hour of the bath is time suspended, when you lie back to contemplate and to dream—a sublimely restorative and relaxing part of the day. Occasionally, you might be inclined to share the experience. French tubs lend themselves to bathing *à deux*, and it is here that baths become a sensual delight. Given the warm water relaxing and caressing both of you, the slippery, scented soaps and oils and the close proximity of two attracted bodies, the bath's power as an aphrodisiac is not hard to understand.

The concept of the bath as treatment derives from the long European tradition of health spas, with their special waters and bathing "cures." Two standard cures, *aromathérapie*—treatments with plant vapors—and *balnéothérapie*—bath treatments—can be reproduced in your own tub. The combined benefits of plants and water will go a long way toward soothing what ails you. You can add extracts of herbs to relax you (pine

157

or camomile), to clear a stuffy head or congested chest (eucalyptus or peppermint) or to revitalize you (rosemary or thyme); you can add oil to condition dry skin; you can add baking soda to calm sunburn and relieve itch; and you can add linden flower or orange blossoms to help you sleep.

Baths relax you through the combined effect of water and warmth. The blood vessels dilate, stimulating circulation, with a general decongestant effect on the body; tight muscles release their tension. You can further enhance the relaxing qualities of your bath, using the following techniques and tips:

Don't step straight into a hot bath. Instead, get into a tub half full of warm water, then turn on the hot water and let it fill the rest of the way. This way, with the body adjusting gradually to the rising temperature, the heat is not a shock.

Try a short massage while you are in the bath, concentrating on the soles of your feet, the palms of your hands and the back of your neck. Do the massage either with your hands or with a shower attachment, with which you can create your own little mini-Jacuzzi. (A shower attachment is also practical for rinsing your hair if you wash it in the bath, and for a quick, cool body rinse at the end of your bath.)

To relax your mind as well as your body, close your eyes and imagine yourself floating free and weightless on a cloud.

After a long, hot bath, wrap yourself up snugly and rest for at least fifteen minutes, to really benefit from the penetrating warmth.

Setting Up the Perfect Bath

Your bathroom decor should be as tranquil as possible to soothe and relax you. Avoid bright colors and strong, harsh lights. Pale pinks, beiges, apricots, soft blue and lavender work well, with accents of green from live, lush plants. Choose the lighting carefully; avoid fluorescent light. Small, theatrical makeup lights are just right, particularly if they are attached to a dimmer. Pure-white globe lights work well too, as do pink bulbs in translucent fixtures. And candles are a wonderful touch if you have a place to put them.

What Every Well-Equipped Bath Should Have

- Soaps—big, generous bars in several colors and fragrances to use according to your mood.
- Scents—an assortment of little sachets of herbs and/or flowers (rose petals, lavender, camomile, rosemary, orange blossoms, thyme, potpourri) to let steep in the bath water while it's running.
- Oils—several fragrant oils, perhaps essences of your favorite perfumes, to pour into the bath water to smooth and lubricate your skin.
- Bubble bath—Vitabath, Obao, or one of the many foaming bath products put out by the perfume companies. *Note:* You would not, of course, use bubble bath, bath oil and floral sachets at the same time. It's just nice to have them all on hand so that you can make a choice according to your needs and your mood.
- Equipment—a large, natural sponge; a pumice stone for feet and other rough areas; a natural scrub glove, such as a loofah; a long-handled brush for your back; an inflatable cushion for your neck.

The bath in France is a ritual, a refuge, a cure.

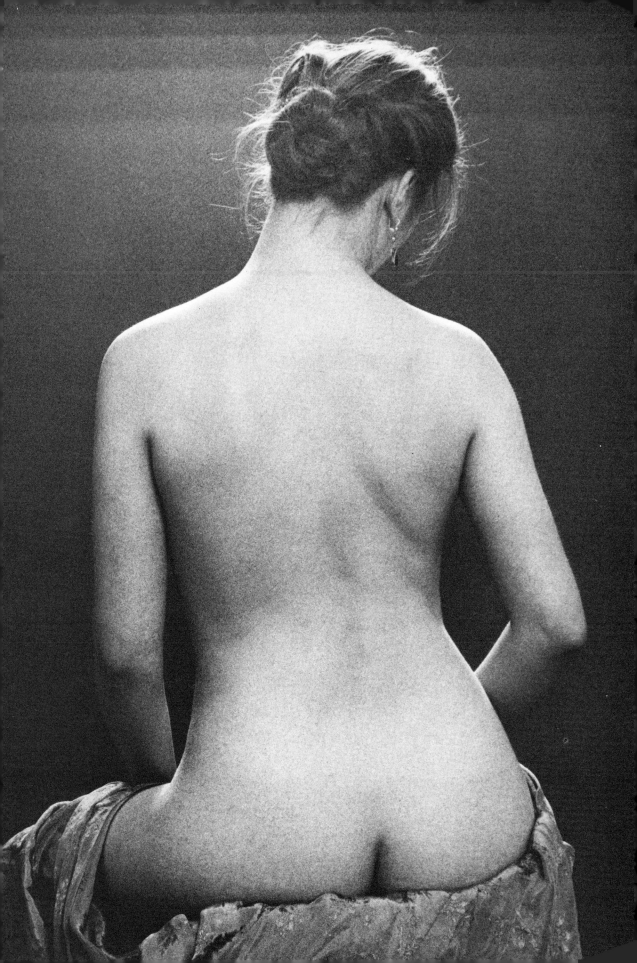

- Lotions—an after-bath body lotion, and a thicker, more occlusive cream for your hands and feet.
- Towels and terry bathrobe—warmed, if possible, on a radiator, or between the folds of an electric blanket.
- Stool—or small tray stand, to keep by the tub, for holding all your bath supplies, as well as reading material, and perhaps a beverage like tea or juice.

Bath Concoctions

The Herbier de Provence recommends two concoctions to brew up yourself and add to the bath water. One is a camomile bath, to calm you, and the other is a rosemary bath, to revitalize you. Both are prepared the same way: Bring two cups of water to a boil, then add either four camomile tea bags or three tablespoons of rosemary. Let boil for five minutes. Strain through cheesecloth or a paper coffee filter. Pour the extract into running bath water.

Bath Temperature

The temperature of the bath water determines the type of bath it is, and what it does for you. One French woman told me that bath water at exactly 98.6 degrees—body temperature—was the most relaxing, since it was the same temperature as the womb and would transport you back, albeit briefly, to that lost, perfect state. In general, a toning, energizing bath is one below 98.6, and a relaxing, sedative bath is one above 98.6.

L'Art du Bain—The Art of the Bath—is a lovely booklet put out by Rochas Perfumes in Paris, in which baths at various temperatures are described:

From 77 to 86 Degrees—this is a refreshing, stimulating bath, especially good in the morning. It should be kept fairly short, about ten minutes. If you don't have a thermometer, the water at this temperature will feel cool, but not cold to the touch.

From 86 to 95 Degrees—a soothing bath that helps you unwind,

calming the nerves and muscles. It's best in the early evening. Water at this temperature will feel almost lukewarm.

At 98.6 Degrees—this is the ideal bath temperature, not too warm, not too cold, very relaxing for the body. Coming from the faucet, the water will feel just slightly warm.

From 104 Degrees Up—this is a very warm or hot bath, which can be used to treat muscular cramps or other body aches. Body creams penetrate well afterward, since pores are wide open. Hot baths should be taken in the evening, and should not last more than fifteen minutes. You should not take a hot bath more than three times a week, since too much water at this temperature tends to slacken the tissue and dilate the blood vessels. Avoid a hot bath entirely if you suffer from hypertension or varicose veins.

The Rochas *L'Art du Bain* goes on to offer several other bath suggestions:

- To relax your eyes while you lie in the tub, place cotton balls saturated with cold camomile tea over your eyes for five minutes.
- Do a few gentle stretching and limbering exercises in the tub: stretch

163

out one leg, then the other, foot flexed, five times. Then rotate feet clockwise, and then counterclockwise, ten times. Repeat the stretches and rotations with your arms, flexing your hands during the stretches.

- Rub the pumice stone gently over your feet and elbows to remove dead, dry skin.
- Never use an electric appliance while you are in the tub. Consequences could be shocking.
- After your bath, rinse yourself with a cool shower; this will wash away the last trace of soap, close the pores and leave you with a rosy glow.

A Total Body Relaxation Program

For the health of your body and mind, it is essential, from time to time, to give yourself a session of total relaxation. Perhaps you've had a terrible, traumatizing day. Or maybe you're simply feeling down, draggy and exhausted, and you're obliged to go out and be "up and bright." Anytime you want to renew yourself body and soul, try this bath-centered, self-help relaxation program, recommended and followed by Ingrid Millet.

What you need:

- Aromatic oil, or five bags of camomile or linden tea
- Cleansing and toning lotions
- Revitalizing facial mask
- Orange juice or warm tea with honey
- Facial moisturizer
- Moisturizing body cream
- Six large pillows
- Two small pillows

What you do:

1. Run a warm, but not hot, bath, adding the aromatic oil or bags of herbal tea to the bath water.

2. While the bath water is running, wash your hands and clean your face with cleansing lotion, followed by the toning lotion. Now apply a stimulating, "wake up" mask to your face and neck.

3. Place a glass of cold orange juice or warm tea on a small stool next to the tub. You'll enjoy sipping either while you lie in the bath.

4. If you like, put on some low, mellow music. (Ingrid Millet, however, prefers to take her bath to the accompaniment of pure silence.)

5. Now enter the tub, lie back and think of nothing except exactly what you are doing: concentrate on the feeling of the water, the sound of the music (or the silence) and the taste of the juice. Stay in the tub about fifteen minutes.

6. Rinse yourself well. Remove the mask. Step out of the tub, dry yourself thoroughly, then apply toning lotion and moisturizer to your face and a rich, moisturizing body lotion to the rest of you.

7. Turn off the lights and put yourself to bed, which you have arranged in the following way:

Your body should be in this position: Prop up two large pillows for your back and a smaller one on top for the back of your neck. Place two more large pillows on top of each other to support your knees, and a

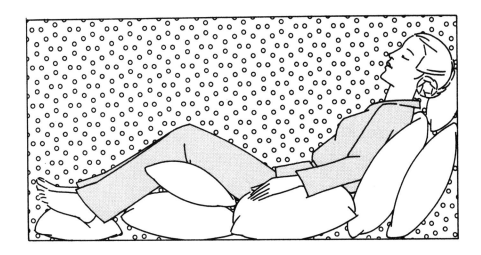

small pillow at the foot of the bed to support your heels. Finally, place a large pillow on each side of you to support your arms. All these pillows create the feeling of lying back in a large, reclining *fauteuil*. With your neck, back, knees, heels and arms supported, you are in the ideal position for relaxation.

8. If your eyes are tired, put cotton squares, soaked in cool camomile tea, or even in plain water, over your lids.

9. Have no music or, if you must, very gentle, very low music. Breathe slowly and deeply and try to think of nothing.

10. Remain in this maximum relaxation position for thirty minutes. Then get up, get dressed and go on with your day. You will feel beautiful, serene and totally refreshed.

VII

PUTTING IT ALL
TOGETHER

"There is no magic formula for beauty," said the late Maria Carita, in an interview I had with her several months before she died. A brusque, blond, warmhearted woman, Maria was beloved and respected in the *haute* worlds of Paris beauty and fashion. She was a creative, brilliant innovator, and her word was gospel. "To be beautiful, to stay beautiful, takes perseverance and discipline," she told me. "All of the great beauties have these qualities. You cannot get by with beauty treatments sporadically, once or twice a year, if you want to be truly well-groomed. You must work out your own beauty routine, caring for yourself daily, weekly and monthly, at home and at the salon, and follow it religiously."

Taking care of yourself means not only keeping your face clean and moisturized, and your hair trimmed and conditioned, but also grooming your hands, feet, legs, breasts and neck, exercising, eating intelligently and relaxing. In the previous chapters I've discussed the Paris way of caring for various parts of your body individually. Now it's time to put it all together. Here is a chart which outlines the basics for caring for your whole self, daily, weekly and monthly. The daily requirements may look time-consuming at first glance, but in fact they will take up only forty to sixty minutes of your day, depending on your hairstyle, makeup and exercise needs.

169

The French woman is profoundly and joyously feminine.

A TOTAL BODY CARE CHART

	Daily	Weekly	Monthly
Face	Cleanse morning and evening; moisturize morning and evening; spray-mist two or three times a day; Beatrice Braun under-eye massage; *10 minutes*	Supplementary mask	Salon or at-home facial
Hair	Brush-and-go style, five minutes; or chignon; *20 minutes*	Wash and condition two or three times a week	Haircut or trim every six weeks
Neck	Clean and moisturize with face morning and evening; Lancray firming exercise; *2 minutes*	When applying supplementary mask to your face, also apply to neck	
Breasts	Cold-water rinse in the shower; Clarins toning exercises; *5 minutes*		

Hips	Braun anticellulite exercises; *10 minutes*		
Legs	Avoid constricting clothing; (to alleviate varicose veins, Institut des Jambes exercises; *10 minutes*		
Arms	Firming exercises; *7 minutes*		
Hands	Moisturize; file nails whenever necessary	Change polish	Manicure
Feet	Marelia routine; *2minutes*	Change polish	Pedicure
Makeup	Olivier Echaudemaison basic makeup; *5 minutes*; or Progressive Makeup; *20 minutes*		
Diet	Drink lots of water, two quarts a day if possible; avoid sugar, starches, salt and alcohol.		Maigrir, Rester Mince thirty-day diet, if necessary

Perfect Scents—the Art of Perfume

The French woman has a special and very personal relationship with her perfumes. She chooses usually two, or perhaps three, scents which complement her personality and style, and she is faithful to them for life. She feels no need to change scents with the seasons. She has one scent for day, a richer and more exotic scent for evening and possibly a very light, fruity or spicy *eau de toilette* for the country or sports. For her friends and family, the scent becomes the woman and the woman becomes the scent.

If you have not yet found the perfumes that are "you," buy several tiny vials of fragrances that please you and try them all out. Your choice is enormous: there are *woody scents*—Chanel #19, Amazone by Hérmès, First by Van Cleef and Arpel, Coeur Joie by Nina Ricci; *spicy scents*—"Y" by Saint-Laurent, Ho-Hang by Balenciaga, Vivara by Pucci, Parure by Guerlain, Sikkim by Lancôme; *citrus-y scents*—Bigarade by Nina Ricci, Eau de Quartz by Molyneux, Eau de Fraîcheur by Revillon; *herbal scents*—Yatagan by Caron, Vent Vert by Balmain; *exotic Oriental scents*—Shalimar and Jicky by Guerlain, Bal à Versailles by Jean Desprez, Chloé by Karl Lagerfeld; and, of course, *floral scents*—Diorissimo by Dior, Rive Gauche by Saint-Laurent, Chamade by Guerlain, Jolie Madame by Balmain, Fidgi by Guy Laroche, Calandre by Paco Rabanne, Fleurs Fraîches by Worth and Audace by Rochas.

There is no formula for finding the right perfume, just as there is no formula for finding the right man. It just happens. As soon as you put on the scent meant for you, you'll know it. For me it was Mitsouko by Guerlain. I fell in love with it when I was fourteen and I've been wearing it ever since. Once you have found your perfect scent, apply it lavishly. Some French women use atomizers and spray themselves entirely with a cloud of perfume—their hair, their clothes, everything! If you put on your perfume with your fingertips, put it all over—your temples, your neck, earlobes, wrists, elbows, between your breasts, on the back of your knees, on the hem of your skirt (so that the fragrance floats around you as you walk), the collar of your blouse, even the lining of your coat.

A word about perfume and the sun: the combination of exotic oils and alcohol from perfumes and the rays of the sun can result in dark splotches on the skin in the areas where you have dabbed your fragrance. The spots can take months to fade. If you are going to be sunbathing, or spending a lot of time exposed to the sun, it would be wise to avoid applying any perfume at all to your skin.

The Total Look, À La Française

The Parisian woman's chic is a combination of simple elements which separately do not seem extraordinary, but together make for a very refined, *soignée* appearance. Her hair is kept neat and her makeup is, of course, carefully applied. But above all, the secret is in the fine points. Salon owner Claude Maxime told me that the Parisian women look so good because they demand perfection in everything—in the fit of their clothes, in the fabrics, in the accessories. To be well turned out simply takes a little more time and attention to detail. Here are some guidelines to help you put yourself together as well as the lovely *Parisiennes* do:

Fabrics

The French woman likes her clothes in natural, high-quality fabrics—wool, silk, cotton, linen. She prefers to spend her clothes money on a few really good items that will last years, rather than a closetful of low-quality, inexpensive goods.

Fit

In Paris, clothes are carefully tailored. The fit is generally a little closer to the body than we are used to, snugger at the shoulders, waist and hips. The length of hems, pants and sleeves varies with the style of the garment, but in general: Sleeves should reach a quarter inch below your wristbone. Most pants should meet the middle of your instep with shoes on, although narrow-legged evening pants are worn shorter, just reaching the anklebone, to expose high, strappy sandals. Skirts are worn one to five inches below the knee, depending mainly on what feels comfortable to the individual (the tendency, however, is toward shorter lengths). Shoulder pads are back, a look that can be quite flattering and slimming, elongating the torso and making the hips look narrower. Blouses and jackets with shoulder pads are often cut larger and softer

176

than their traditional counterparts. Some jackets are worn looser on the body, others have fitted waists with peplums. The look is dramatic, very forties, a style the French call *retro*.

Stockings

The right stocking for your outfit and shoes is a subtle detail important to your total look. The shade should be in harmony with your clothes—brown/beige shades for clothes in the red-yellow-green-brown family, and grey, taupy shades or sheerest black for clothes in the rose-blue-grey-black family. Or match your outfit with a sheer stocking in exactly the same shade as the fabric. If you wear sandals, be sure to wear sandalfoot stockings, without heel or toe reinforcement. To find exactly the right shade of stocking for a particular ensemble, take along a small swatch of the fabric when you shop for the stockings.

To accompany high-heeled pumps, sheer stockings with seams, in grey, brown or blue, are making a small comeback, along with lacy garter belts. It's an old style that looks and feels supersexy, guaranteed to transform any woman into a *femme fatale*.

Shoes

Parisiennes favor high-heeled shoes and boots, which give a longer, more elegant look to the leg. A three-inch heel may not be made for serious walking, but it's good-looking and feminine. If you want to try out this sophisticated, sexy look, why not buy one versatile pair—such as low-cut, high-heeled black pumps—and see what they do for your clothes. Or try a high-heeled, strappy, patent leather sandal, a shoe you can wear out at night all year round. Open-toe pumps are appearing again in Paris, with the return of the forties look, and the trend may well cut into the popularity of the sandal, particularly for daytime.

Accessories

Accessories can make or break your total look, so choose them carefully.

Handbags, for daytime, should be neat and practical, but not enormous. A pouch shoulder bag or a large, flat clutch are good choices. If you have a great deal of paraphernalia to carry with you, put it in a roomy attaché case or a leather or canvas tote. Avoid handbags with handles to slip over your wrist or forearm. They look dated. Do *not* carry your everyday bag when you're all dressed up. It looks frumpy. For evening, the tinier the bag the better, either clutch-style, or on a long cord, chain or ribbon, to wear on your shoulder, around your neck, or bandolier-style across your torso.

Jewelry should be simple and striking. Scatter pins, used with imagination and humor, are seen around Paris both for daytime and evening decoration. The pins, usually two or three together, are attached to collars, jacket lapels, décolleté necklines, cuffs and ribbons or ties at the waist. With the *retro* look, large brooches are worn just below the shoulder. Earrings are perennially popular, with the trend now toward the delicate, dangling variety, or large clips worn with the hair in a chignon. Pearls, single or double medium-length strands, are enjoying a renaissance, and look super with silk.

Scarves are indispensable to the *Parisiennes*. They have wardrobes of scarves—large, small, squares, oblongs, wool, silk, daytime and evening. A scarf can put the finishing touch, the final brushstroke, on your outfit. Experiment with scarves: tie the knot at various lengths; try two scarves together, a small one around your neck, a larger one draped over your shoulders; wear a large scarf, perhaps a pretty challis print, over one shoulder, tying one end to your belt in the front, the other end to your belt in the back; or drape a long, oblong scarf, in a solid, neutral shade, under the collar and over the lapels of your blazer. With a solid-color daytime or evening suit, tie two floaty chiffon oblong scarves in a half-bow at your throat, the looped half arranged over your shoulder, the loose half hanging straight down. This is a feminine touch innovated by Saint Laurent to soften the strict lines of a fitted suit.

The French woman enjoys taking time for herself, and making an effort to be the most attractive woman she can be. She is meticulous and exacting, a perfectionist to the core. She cares for and clothes her body to please herself, and to please her men. These qualities may not further France's feminist movement, but they are fundamental to the French woman's reputation as the most womanly woman in the world. She is profoundly and joyously feminine.

VIII
Appendix

A Guide to Featured Paris Beauty Establishments

Patrick Alès
37 avenue Franklin Roosevelt
75008 Paris
Tel: 225-57-49

Alexandre
120 rue du Faubourg
    Saint-Honoré
75008 Paris
Tel.: 359-40-09

Béatrice Braun
39 rue de Sèvres
75006 Paris
Tel. 544-19-34

Carita
11 rue du Faubourg
    Saint-Honoré
75008 Paris
Tel.: 265-79-00

Clarins
35 rue Tronchet
75008 Paris
Tel.: 265-30-70

Jacques Clemente
Elizabeth Arden
59 avenue Marceau
75016 Paris
Tel.: 720-02-02

Olivier Echaudemaison
Harriet Hubbard-Ayer
120 rue du Faubourg
    Saint-Honoré
75008 Paris
Tel.: 225-2108

Jean-Pierre Fleurimon
71 avenue Marceau
75116 Paris
Tel.: 720-49-61

Jacques France
122 rue du Faubourg
    Saint-Honoré
75008 Paris
Tel.: 225-91-12

Louis G.
4 rue de Bourgogne
75007 Paris
Tel.: 551-30-39

Guerlain
68 avenue des Champs-Elysées
75008 Paris
Tel.: 359-3110

Herbier de Provence
19 rue du Jour
75001 Paris
Tel.: 508-89-84

Institut des Jambes
87 rue St. Lazare
75009 Paris
Tel.: 280-56-33

Isabelle Lancray
29 rue François Ier
75008 Paris
Tel.: 359-83-08

Luis Llongueras
229 rue Saint-Honoré
75001 Paris
Tel.: 260-6448

José Luis
Charles of the Ritz-Saint Laurent
28-34 boulevard du Parc
92521 Neuilly-sur-Seine
Tel.: 326-47-64 or 747-11-90

Maigrir, Rester Mince
46 rue Blanche
75009 Paris
Tel.: 280-30-40

Jean-Marc Maniatis
35 rue de Sèvres
75006 Paris
Tel.: 544-16-39

Marelia
Institut Payot
10 rue Castiglione
75001 Paris
Tel.: 260-32-87

Claude Maxime
15 avenue Kléber
75116 Paris
Tel.: 740-91-00

Ingrid Millet
54 rue du Faubourg
  Saint-Honoré
75008 Paris
Tel.: 266-66-20

To be beautiful takes perserverance and discipline.